W9-CBX-469

NOW IS YOUR TIME!

Colored orphanage in New York, 1860. *New-York Historical Society*

WALTER DEAN MYERS

NOW IS YOUR TIME!

The African-American Struggle for Freedom

HarperCollins*Publishers*

By the same author

SCORPIONS
A Newbery Honor Book

THE MOUSE RAP

Now Is Your Time!
The African-American Struggle for Freedom
Copyright © 1991 by Walter Dean Myers
All rights reserved.
No part of this book may be used or reproduced
in any manner whatsoever without written permission
except in the case of brief quotations
embodied in critical articles and reviews.
Printed in the United States of America.
For information address HarperCollins Children's Books,
a division of HarperCollins Publishers,
10 East 53rd Street, New York, NY 10022.

2   3   4   5   6   7   8   9   10

Library of Congress Cataloging-in-Publication Data
Myers, Walter Dean, date
   Now is your time! : the African-American struggle for freedom / by
Walter Dean Myers.
      p.   cm.
   Summary: A history of the African-American struggle for freedom
and equality, beginning with the capture of Africans in 1619,
continuing through the American Revolution, the Civil War, and into
contemporary times.
   ISBN 0-06-024370-8. — ISBN 0-06-024371-6 (lib. bdg.)
   1. Afro-Americans—History—Juvenile literature.   [1. Afro-
Americans—History.]   I. Title.
E185.M96   1991   91-314
973′.0496073—dc20   CIP
                                                                      AC

To Theodore Brunson, Charles L. Blockson,
Howard Dodson, Debra Newman Ham, William W. Layton,
William Miles, Clement Price, Dorothy Provine,
Paul E. Sluby, and to all those
who recognize the importance
of preserving and protecting
their own history.

Acknowledgments

Writing this book has been at times extremely pleasurable and at other times extremely hard work. The work has been eased considerably by the cooperation of institutions and individuals who have given generously of their time and resources, and I would like to take this opportunity to thank them.

First there are the people I have had the opportunity to interview: Winifred Latimer Norman; Solomon C. Fuller; Cheryl Henderson Brown; and Linda Brown, whose families are so vital a part of American history.

The work could not have been done without access to previous research, and the following provided access to their collections: The University of West Virginia Collection; The George Peabody Library, Baltimore; the Mount Vernon Ladies' Association; the Maryland Historical Society; the Schomburg Research Library of the New York Public Library; and the Jersey City Public Library. I would like to thank Don C. Wood, and especially Dr. Edward Robinson of Philadelphia, for their insights into history. I would like to express my appreciation to my editor, Linda Zuckerman, for her forbearance. I want to thank my sisters, Geraldine, Viola, Ethel, and Imogene, for their help in constructing the oral history of our family. Finally I would like to thank my wife, Constance, who somehow always manages to tolerate my lack of patience.

Contents

According to an African tradition among the people of Abron-Gyaman (Ivory Coast), a drummer must recite the following words before giving information to the village.

Every word is the word;
the word is easy
and difficult.
He who would speak
must speak clearly
and must speak the truth.

I bring as much truth as I know.

Walter Dean Myers
1991

1

The Land

To understand the story of the African-American experience, we have to begin with the land. North America, incredibly rich and beautiful, stretching forever westward from the shores of the Atlantic Ocean, was irresistible. There were mountain ranges through which rivers coursed, bringing minerals to the lush valleys and plains below. That the climate was right for agriculture was evident from the crops of the brown- and copper-skinned people we call Native Americans today.

For Europe it was the age of exploration. Kings and queens, wealthy merchants, sometimes even private individuals, hired ships to travel the world. They were chiefly looking for faster trade routes to the Far East and new sources of gold, silver, and spices. What they found in their travels westward was the land that would one day become the United States.

Living on this land were many different groups of peoples: The Navaho were largely nomadic, constantly on the move, while the Seneca had lived in a relatively small area of the northeast for hundreds of years. Toward the middle of the continent the Erie Indians lived in the area of the Great Lakes. The Seminole were largely in the southeast, while in the southwest the Hopi built three- and four-story structures, sometimes with hundreds of rooms.

These peoples had lived on this land with their villages, their governments, their beliefs, and their customs, for thousands of years.

The Europeans called the land North *America*, after the Italian explorer Amerigo Vespucci. Earlier Christopher Columbus, an explorer sailing under the flag of Spain, had reached the island of San Salvador, south of Florida, and had called the people he found there "Indians." Soon the Europeans were calling all the peoples of North America Indians.

While some explorers were crossing the Atlantic Ocean, others, such as Diogo Cão and Bartholomeu Dias of Portugal, were making important discoveries along the west coast of Africa.

Griots—African storytellers—speak of African kingdoms that stretch back hundreds of years before the birth of Christ. By the ninth century the religion of Islam had spread its influence among the early inhabitants of ancient Ghana. The kingdom of Ghana gave way to that of Mali, with its center of learning at Timbuktu and the beginnings of the gold trade across the Sahara Desert, and by the end of the fifteenth century, Sunni Ali Ber and Askia Muhammad I, the great leaders of the powerful

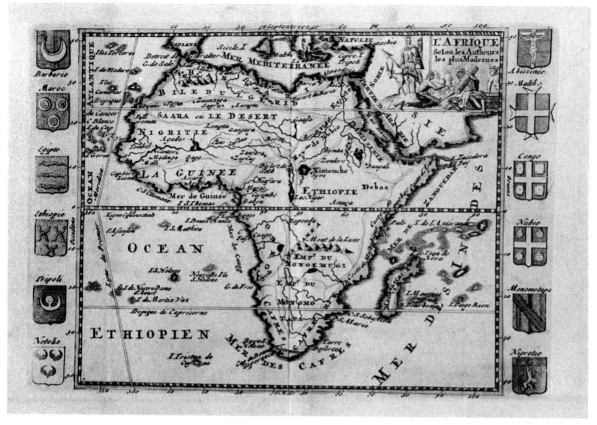

French map of Africa, 1708. *Author*

Songhai Empire, were legendary figures.

In the 1400's, long caravans of traders made their way from the forests of the Yoruba across the continent to Egypt in east Africa. Merchants from France, England, India, and Holland traded for African gold and ivory in crowded north-African markets. But sub-Saharan Africa was cut off from Europe by the desert.

In the early sixteenth century, when Europeans began to explore the world by ship, the riches of the west African coast were discovered. Soon Portuguese, Spanish, Dutch, and English com-

Land grants such as this were given on condition that the person receiving the grant bring either slaves or indentured servants to the colony to work the land. The land granted here was later bought by George Washington. *Mount Vernon Ladies' Association*

panies began to build trading posts along the coast. They also sought colonies in what they called the "New World."

In 1584 the Englishman Walter Raleigh started such a colony on the eastern coast of North America in a place he called Virginia. The early colonists found no cities in North America to rival those in Great Britain and Europe. What they did find was a land of richness and beauty and the possibility of enormous wealth that free land promised.

English, Dutch, and Spanish settlements sprang up along the east coast of North America, while smaller Spanish and French settlements appeared in the west. English settlements were named Virginia, Delaware, and Maryland. New Amsterdam was Dutch, and Florida was claimed by the Spanish.

The largest tracts of land were settled by the British, who sent hundreds of settlers to the southern part of the continent with offers of free land for people who would promise to develop it. The idea, of course, was that the people developing the land would be British, and so the British Empire, already the largest in the world, would continue to grow.

In a world in which most people survived by farming, the land grants were extremely attractive. America was described by many as the best poor man's country in the world. The cost of buying land in America was less than the annual taxes would have been on the same land if it had been in England.

Typical in many ways of the early American colonists were two English brothers, William and John Dandridge. William, a handsome, self-assured man with a great sense of presence, was an officer in the Royal Navy. Young John, only fourteen years old but bright and ambitious like his brother, was still looking for a profession. They left behind another brother, Bartholomew Dandridge, who became a noted portrait painter. His paintings are on display in the National Portrait Gallery in London.

The opportunities for the Dandridges, had they remained in England, were only fair; in America, with hard work and inexpensive land, they might make their fortunes. Around the year

William Dandridge, 1689–1743, along with his brother John, came to the colonies to seek his fortune. *Virginia Historical Society*

1711, uncertain of what life would be like in the largely unpopulated land, they decided to try their luck. William Dandridge settled in Virginia, near the Pamunkey River; John would later build a house nearby on the other side of the same river.

The Dandridges, like many colonists who came to North

America, were to become closely entangled with the lives of the Africans who were brought there. Through the course of this book we will follow their story over the years.

The land was plentiful and rich, but who would work it? It didn't make sense for a colonist to work for somebody else when land down the road could be had for practically nothing. It became clear that what was needed in the new colonies was a new supply of laborers whose ambitions could be limited.

One of the first solutions was to bring more people from Great Britain. Poor people in England and Ireland who owed money they could not repay were forced to come to the colonies and work for nothing until their debts were paid off. Occasionally people would agree to work for a certain amount of time in return for their passage to the new world and their chance at America's wealth. Prisoners, as well, were often sent on the ships that left Liverpool and other English ports for the east coast of America.

How long people had to work depended on their circumstances. A criminal might have to work for fourteen or more years, while a person just paying for passage might have to work for only four years before the passage was paid for.

When the amount of time was settled, a contract was drawn up and then carefully torn in half. The worker took one half and the person for whom he or she had to work took the other. The pieces could be matched where the paper was torn or "indented," and these workers were called "indentured servants." When their time was up, the servants—men, women, and often children—were given the other half of the indenture and were free to go their own way.

Indentures could be bought and sold. Wealthier colonists, looking for laborers, would go to the docks when a ship arrived to buy the indentures by paying the original contract holder the value of the passage plus a small bonus.

Indentured labor helped, but did not solve, the problem. The need for labor was much greater than the flow of servants from Europe. The labor had to be found elsewhere.

It was common practice among warring African nations that prisoners taken in battle were held in captivity for long periods of time. Sometimes they would be used as hostages against future attack, or sent back to their original people in exchange for goods. African chiefs who were captured in battle were frequently ransomed or exchanged for other prisoners. The prisoners would become part of the community of their captors. It was not unusual for a man to be taken prisoner and then later rise to a prominent position with his new people. Sometimes prisoners faced a lifetime of servitude.

The European traders eyed the captives they saw among the Africans. Seeing an opportunity to solve the labor problem in the colonies, they began to trade their goods for African prisoners, and in 1619 the first African captives were brought to Virginia.

At first, when both Africans and indentured whites were being brought to the colonies, there was little difference in the attitudes toward them. But the laws of Great Britain, under which the most populous colonies lived, protected the indentured servants by clearly stating how much time they had to

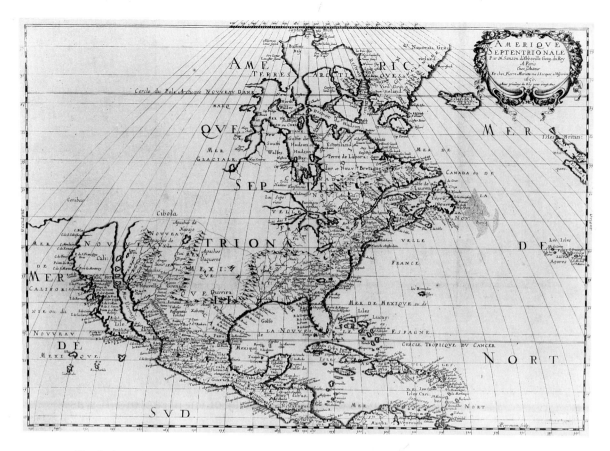

North America as known by Europeans in 1650. The western coast had not been sufficiently explored to be included on this French-made map. *Library of Congress*

serve and declaring their children to be free. No such system protected the African captives.

Some of the first Africans brought to this country were eventually freed under laws similar to indenture laws; most were not. Gradually those areas of the country that used the labor of African captives made laws saying that they would have to serve for as long as they lived; what's more, their "increase," or children, would also have to serve forever. In other words, the Africans "belonged" to whoever held them captive.

Once the trade in Africans started, it increased quickly. There was an enormous profit to be made in sending ships to Africa and transporting a human cargo across the Atlantic Ocean to the West Indies and the southern colonies, and some of the colonists were eager to exploit it.

The raids on west Africa that supplied North America with labor would last for some 236 years, from 1619 to 1855, long after the legal importation of Africans had ended. During that time the terrible trade in human beings plunged west Africa into chaos. Europeans brought their guns into the ports of Africa and attacked small villages. They provided weapons for Africans who were willing—sometimes to avoid slavery themselves but often out of pure greed—to start wars against their neighbors in order to supply captives for the waiting ships. Local governments fell, unable to defend their people against European guns. Entire villages were forced to leave their traditional lands to avoid the manufactured wars.

America was a land where people who had been poor could become rich. All that was needed was land and labor. The early colonists were willing to take the land from the Native Americans and the labor from the African captives.

2

Abd al-Rahman Ibrahima

Who were these Africans being brought to the New World? What was their African world like? There is no single answer. The Africans came from many countries, and from many cultures. Like the Native Americans, they established their territories based on centuries of tradition. Most, but not all, of the Africans who were brought to the colonies came from central and west Africa. Among them was a man named Abd al-Rahman Ibrahima.

The European invaders, along with those Africans who cooperated with them, had made the times dangerous. African nations that had lived peacefully together for centuries now eyed each other warily. Slight insults led to major battles. Bands of outlaws roamed the countryside attacking the small villages, kidnaping those unfortunate enough to have wandered from the protection of their people. The stories that came from the coast were frightening. Those kidnaped were taken to the sea and sold to whites, put on boats, and taken across the sea. No one knew what happened then.

Abd al-Rahman Ibrahima was born in 1762 in Fouta Djallon, a district of the present country of Guinea. It is a beautiful land of green mountains rising majestically from grassy plains, a land rich with minerals, especially bauxite.

Ibrahima was a member of the powerful and influential Fula people and a son of one of their chieftains. The religion of Islam had swept across Africa centuries before, and the young Ibrahima was raised in the tradition of the Moslems.

The Fula were taller and lighter in complexion than the other inhabitants of Africa's west coast; they had silky hair, which they often wore long. A pastoral people, the Fula had a complex system of government, with the state divided into nine provinces and each province divided again into smaller districts. Each province had its chief and its subchiefs.

As the son of a chief Ibrahima was expected to assume a role of political leadership when he came of age. He would also be expected to set a moral example, and to be well versed in his religion. When he reached twelve he was sent to Timbuktu to study.

Under the Songhai dynasty leader Askia the Great, Timbuktu had become a center of learning and one of the largest cities in the Songhai Empire. The young Ibrahima knew he was privileged to attend the best-known school in west Africa. Large and

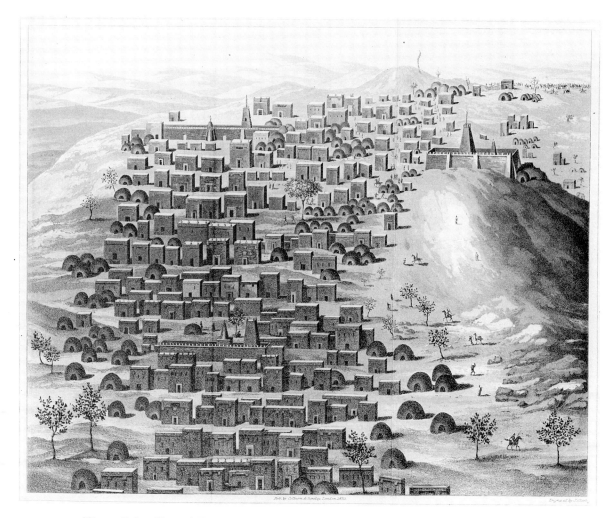

View of the City of Timbuktu where, as a young man, Ibrahima studied the Koran. *Library of Congress*

sophisticated, with wide, tree-lined streets, the city attracted scholars from Africa, Europe, and Asia. Islamic law, medicine, and mathematics were taught to the young men destined to become the leaders of their nations. It was a good place for a young man to be. The city was well guarded, too. It had to be, to prevent the chaos that, more and more, dominated African life nearer the coast.

Ibrahima learned first to recite from the Koran, the Moslem holy book, and then to read it in Arabic. From the Koran, it was felt, came all other knowledge. After Ibrahima had finished his studies in Timbuktu, he returned to Fouta Djallon to continue to prepare himself to be a chief.

The Fula had little contact with whites, and what little contact they did have was filled with danger. So when, in 1781, a white man claiming to be a ship's surgeon stumbled into one of their villages, they were greatly surprised.

John Coates Cox hardly appeared to be a threat. A slight man, blind in one eye, he had been lost for days in the forested regions bordering the mountains. He had injured his leg, and it had become badly infected as he tried to find help. By the time he was found and brought to the Fula chiefs, he was more dead than alive.

Dr. Cox, an Irishman, told of being separated from a hunting party that had left from a ship on which he had sailed as ship's surgeon. The Fula chief decided that he would help Cox. He was taken into a hut, and a healer was assigned the task of curing his infected leg.

During the months Dr. Cox stayed with the Fula, he met Ibrahima, now a tall, brown-skinned youth who had reached manhood. His bearing reflected his status as the son of a major chief. Dr. Cox had learned some Fulani, the Fula language, and the two men spoke. Ibrahima was doubtless curious about the white man's world, and Dr. Cox was as impressed by Ibrahima's education as he had been by the kindness of his people.

14

66752144

When Dr. Cox was well enough to leave, he was provided with a guard; but before he left, he warned the Fula about the danger of venturing too near the ships that docked off the coast of Guinea. The white doctor knew that the ships were there to take captives.

Cox and Ibrahima embraced fondly and said their good-byes, thinking they would never meet again.

Ibrahima married and became the father of several children. He was in his mid-twenties when he found himself leading the Fula cavalry in their war with the Mandingo.

The first battles went well, with the enemy retreating before the advancing Fula. The foot warriors attacked first, breaking the enemy's ranks and making them easy prey for the well-trained Fula cavalry. With the enemy in full rout the infantry returned to their towns while the horsemen, led by Ibrahima, chased the remaining stragglers. The Fula fought their enemies with spears, bows, slings, swords, and courage.

The path of pursuit led along a path that narrowed sharply as the forests thickened. The fleeing warriors disappeared into the forest that covered a sharply rising mountain. Thinking the enemy had gone for good, Ibrahima felt it would be useless to chase them further.

"We could not see them," he would write later.

But against his better judgment, he decided to look for them. The horsemen dismounted at the foot of a hill and began the steep climb on foot. Halfway up the hill the Fula realized they had been lured into a trap! Ibrahima heard the rifles firing, saw the smoke from the powder and the men about him falling to the

15

ground, screaming in agony. Some died instantly. Many horses, hit by the gunfire, thrashed about in pain and panic. The firing was coming from both sides, and Ibrahima ordered his men to the top of the hill, where they could, if time and Allah permitted it, try a charge using the speed and momentum of their remaining horses.

Ibrahima was among the first to mount, and urged his animal onward. The enemy warriors came out of the forests, some with bows and arrows, others with muskets that he knew they had obtained from the Europeans. The courage of the Fula could not match the fury of the guns. Ibrahima called out to his men to save themselves, to flee as they could. Many tried to escape, rushing madly past the guns. Few survived.

Those who did clustered about their young leader, determined to make one last, desperate stand. Ibrahima was hit in the back by an arrow, but the aim was not true and the arrow merely cut his broad shoulder. Then something smashed against his head from the rear.

The next thing Ibrahima knew was that he was choking. Then he felt himself being lifted from water. He tried to move his arms, but they had been fastened securely behind his back. He had been captured.

When he came to his full senses, he looked around him. Those of his noble cavalry who had not been captured were already dead. Ibrahima was unsteady on his legs as his clothes and sandals were stripped from him. The victorious Mandingo warriors now pushed him roughly into file with his men. They began the long trek that would lead them to the sea.

16

In Fouta Djallon being captured by the enemy meant being forced to do someone else's bidding, sometimes for years. If you could get a message to your people, you could, perhaps, buy your freedom. Otherwise, it was only if you were well liked, or if you married one of your captor's women, that you would be allowed to go free, or to live like a free person.

Ibrahima sensed that things would not go well for him.

The journey to the sea took weeks. Ibrahima was tied to other men, with ropes around their necks. Each day they walked from dawn to dusk. Those who were slow were knocked brutally to the ground. Some of those who could no longer walk were speared and left to die in agony. It was the lucky ones who were killed outright if they fell.

When they reached the sea, they remained bound hand and foot. There were men and women tied together. Small children clung to their mothers as they waited for the boats to come and the bargaining to begin.

Ibrahima, listening to the conversations of the men who held him captive, could understand those who spoke Arabic. These Africans were a low class of men, made powerful by the guns they had been given, made evil by the white man's goods. But it didn't matter who was evil and who was good. It only mattered who held the gun.

Ibrahima was inspected on the shore, then put into irons and herded into a small boat that took him out to a ship that was larger than any he had ever seen.

The ship onto which Ibrahima was taken was already crowded with black captives. Some shook in fear; others, still tied, fought by hurling their bodies at their captors. The beating and the killing continued until the ones who were left knew that their lot was hopeless.

On board the ship there were more whites with guns, who shoved them toward the open hatch. Some of the Africans hesitated at the hatch, and were clubbed down and pushed below-decks.

It was dark beneath the deck, and difficult to breathe. Bodies were pressed close against other bodies. In the section of the ship he was in, men prayed to various gods in various languages. It seemed that the whites would never stop pushing men into the already crowded space. Two sailors pushed the Africans into position so that each would lie in the smallest space possible. The sailors panted and sweated as they untied the men and then chained them to a railing that ran the length of the ship.

The ship rolled against its mooring as the anchor was lifted, and the journey began. The boards of the ship creaked and moaned as it lifted and fell in the sea. Some of the men got sick, vomiting upon themselves in the wretched darkness. They lay cramped, muscles aching, irons cutting into their legs and wrists, gasping for air.

Once a day they would be brought out on deck and made to jump about for exercise. They were each given a handful of either beans or rice cooked with yams and water from a cask. The white sailors looked hardly better than the Africans, but it was they who held the guns.

Illness and the stifling conditions on the ships caused many deaths. How many depended largely on how fast the ships could

son of a chief. He wanted to offer a ransom for his own release, but Foster wasn't interested. He understood, perhaps from the boy whom he had purchased previously, that this new African was claiming to be an important person. Foster had probably never heard of the Fula or their culture; he had paid good money for the African, and wasn't about to give him up. Foster gave Ibrahima a new name: He called him Prince.

For Ibrahima there was confusion and pain. What was he to do? A few months before, he had been a learned man and a leader among his people. Now he was a captive in a strange land where he neither spoke the language nor understood the customs. Was he never to see his family again? Were his sons forever lost to him?

As a Fula, Ibrahima wore his hair long; Foster insisted that it be cut. Ibrahima's clothing had been taken from him, and his sandals. Now the last remaining symbol of his people, his long hair, had been taken as well.

He was told to work in the fields. He refused, and he was tied and whipped. The sting of the whip across his naked flesh was terribly painful, but it was nothing like the pain he felt within. The whippings forced him to work.

For Ibrahima this was not life, but a mockery of life. There was the waking in the morning and the sleeping at night; he worked, he ate, but this was not life. What was more, he could not see an end to it. It was this feeling that made him attempt to escape.

Ibrahima escaped to the backwoods regions of Natchez. He hid there, eating wild berries and fruit, not daring to show his face to any man, white or black. There was no telling who could be trusted. Sometimes he saw men with dogs and knew they were searching for runaways, perhaps him.

Where was he to run? What was he to do? He didn't know the country, he didn't know how far it was from Fouta Djallon, or how to get back to his homeland. He could tell that this place was ruled by white men who held him in captivity. The other blacks he had seen were from all parts of Africa. Some he recognized by their tribal markings, some he did not. None were allowed to speak their native tongues around the white men. Some already knew nothing of the languages of their people.

As time passed Ibrahima's despair deepened. His choices were simple. He could stay in the woods and probably die, or he could submit his body back into bondage. There is no place in Islamic law for a man to take his own life. Ibrahima returned to Thomas Foster.

Foster still owed money to the man from whom he had purchased Ibrahima. The debt would remain whether he still possessed the African or not. Foster was undoubtedly glad to see that the African had returned. Thin, nearly starving, Ibrahima was put to work.

Ibrahima submitted himself to the will of Thomas Foster. He was a captive, held in bondage not only by Foster but by the society in which he found himself. Ibrahima maintained his beliefs in the religion of Islam and kept its rituals as best he could. He was determined to be the same person he had always been: Abd al-Rahman Ibrahima of Fouta Djallon and of the proud Fula people.

By 1807 the area had become the Mississippi Territory. Ibrahima was forty-five and had been in bondage for twenty years. During those years he met and married a woman whom Foster had purchased, and they began to raise a family. Fouta Djallon was more and more distant, and he had become resigned to the idea that he would never see it or his family again.

Thomas Foster had grown wealthy and had become an important man in the territory. At forty-five Ibrahima was considered old. He was less useful to Foster, who now let the tall African grow a few vegetables on a side plot and sell them in town, since there was nowhere in the territory that the black man could go where he would not be captured by some other white man and returned.

It was during one of these visits to town that Ibrahima saw a white man who looked familiar. The smallish man walked slowly and with a limp. Ibrahima cautiously approached the man and spoke to him. The man looked closely at Ibrahima, then spoke his name. It was Dr. Cox.

The two men shook hands and Dr. Cox, who now lived in the territory, took Ibrahima to his home. John Cox had not prospered over the years, but he was still hopeful. He listened carefully as Ibrahima told his story—the battle near Fouta Djallon, the defeat, the long journey across the Atlantic Ocean, and, finally, his sale to Thomas Foster and the years of labor.

Abd al-Rahman Ibrahima from an engraving by Henry Inman in 1828. Ibrahima's name is written in Arabic, the language he had learned to read and write as a young man in Africa. *Library of Congress*

Dr. Cox and Ibrahima went to the Foster plantation. Meeting with Foster, he explained how he had met the tall black man. Surely, he reasoned, knowing that Ibrahima was of royal blood, Foster would free him? The answer was a firm, but polite, no. No amount of pleading would make Foster change his mind. It didn't matter that Dr. Cox had supported what Ibrahima had told Foster so many years before, that he was a prince. To Foster the man was merely his property.

Dr. Cox had to leave the man whose people had saved his life, but he told Ibrahima that he would never stop working for his freedom.

Andrew Marschalk, the son of a Dutch baker, was a printer, a pioneer in his field, and a man of great curiosity. By the time Marschalk heard about it, Cox had told a great many people in the Natchez district the story of African royalty being held in slavery in America. Marschalk was fascinated. He suggested that Ibrahima write a letter to his people, telling them of his whereabouts and asking them to ransom him. But Ibrahima had not been to his homeland in twenty years. The people there were still being captured by slave traders. He would have to send a messenger who knew the countryside, and who knew the Fula. Where would he find such a man?

For a long time Ibrahima did nothing. Finally, some time after the death of Dr. Cox in 1816, Ibrahima wrote the letter that Marschalk suggested. He had little faith in the procedure but felt he had nothing to lose. Marschalk was surprised when Ibrahima appeared with the letter written neatly in Arabic. Since one place in Africa was the same as the next to Marschalk, he sent the letter not to Fouta Djallon but to Morocco.

The government of Morocco did not know Ibrahima but understood from his letter that he was a Moslem. Moroccan officials, in a letter to President James Monroe, pleaded for the release of Ibrahima. The letter reached Henry Clay, the American Secretary of State.

The United States had recently ended a bitter war with Tripoli in north Africa, and welcomed the idea of establishing good relations with Morocco, another north African country. Clay wrote to Foster about Ibrahima.

Foster resented the idea of releasing Ibrahima. The very idea that the government of Morocco had written to Clay and discussed a religion that Ibrahima shared with other Africans gave Ibrahima a past that Foster had long denied, a past as honorable as Foster's. This idea challenged a basic premise of slavery—a premise that Foster must have believed without reservation: that the Africans had been nothing but savages, with no humanity or human feelings, and therefore it was all right to enslave them. But after more letters and pressure from the State Department, Foster agreed to release Ibrahima if he could be assured that Ibrahima would leave the country and return to Fouta Djallon.

Many people who believed that slavery was wrong also believed that Africans could not live among white Americans. The American Colonization Society had been formed expressly to send freed Africans back to Africa. The society bought land, and a colony called Liberia was established on the west coast of Africa. Foster was assured that Ibrahima would be sent there.

Emigration Record of the American Colonization Society for the ship *Harriet*, showing that "Abduhuli Rahahman," after forty years of American captivity, had finally reached Africa. He died in Liberia before reaching Fouta Djallon. *Library of Congress*

By then Ibrahima's cause had been taken up by a number of abolitionist groups in the north as well as by many free Africans. They raised money to buy his wife's freedom as well.

On February 7, 1829, Ibrahima and his wife sailed on the ship *Harriet* for Africa. The ship reached Liberia, and Ibrahima now had to find a way to reach his people again. He never found that way. Abd al-Rahman Ibrahima died in Liberia in July 1829.

Who was Ibrahima? He was one of millions of Africans taken by force from their native lands. He was the son of a chief, a warrior, and a scholar. But to Ibrahima the only thing that mattered was that he had lost his freedom. If he had been a herder in Fouta Djallon, or an artist in Benin, or a farmer along the Gambia, it would have been the same. Ibrahima was an African who loved freedom no less than other beings on earth. And he was denied that freedom.

3

The Plantation Society

The ships were owned by New England merchants and financed by bankers in Boston and New York and Philadelphia, but the human cargo they brought across the ocean was almost always sent to the large farms in the South. It was to work on these plantations that the Africans were needed. The plantation owners would have people waiting at the shore to see what new Africans were being brought in. Were they free of disease? Were they young? Large plantation owners who had the cash in hand had first choice of the frightened captives. Smaller farmers, like Thomas Foster, who made a down payment and paid the rest when the crops came in, had to wait their turn to bid on the African labor.

Aboard the ships the crews prepared the Africans for sale. They would be made to move around so that they wouldn't

It was quickly learned that Africans could do any sort of work, from building houses such as the Homewood mansion in Mississippi (shown here) to nursing. *Library of Congress*

appear stiff once on shore. Their skin would be oiled to give it a glowing appearance, and any sores would be covered with tar to hide infection. The crew would stand guard, guns at the ready, knowing that once the Africans saw shore, they might rebel.

The Africans would wonder what destiny faced them, and if

they would ever have a chance to return to their homes and families. As they were taken to the shore in chains, to the auction blocks, they would try to look around at the strange country they were in, and at the strange people. They would doubtlessly notice the guns. They would see other Africans who were dressed like the whites and wonder what place they had in this new world. What they would discover was that they were to become an important part of plantation society, which could be roughly divided into four major groups: the wealthy planters, the smaller planters, the poor whites, and the Africans.

Plantations were very large Southern estates on which the workers lived. There was usually a "big house," where the owner of the plantation, or his representative, lived with his family. There would be a place, usually some distance from the big house, where the Africans lived. The "quarters," as this place was called, were often crudely built houses barely serving as shelter from the cold. Sometimes, however, they were at least as good as the homes of poor whites in the area.

The purpose of the plantation was to raise a main crop, usually tobacco, cotton, or rice, which then had to be harvested and sold. With land so cheap, the tendency of most planters was to raise as large a crop as possible without worrying about how the land was being depleted. Because each kind of crop takes different nutrients from the earth, the land has to be given a chance to regain them. Farmers accomplish this by alternating different crops on the land (crop rotation) or by not planting a portion of the land until it has recovered (allowing it to lie fallow).

(In England, where land was limited and therefore very ex-

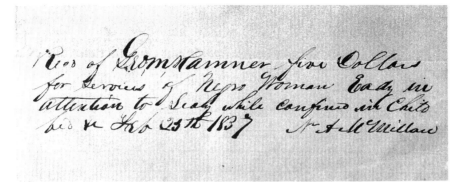

This receipt was for the services of Eady attending Sealy, probably another African woman, in childbirth. The money, of course, went to Eady's owner. *Author*

pensive, land had to be carefully preserved. Often, English farmers visiting America were shocked to see how inefficient most farming was in the American South.)

Plantation owners also tried to grow enough food for their own use. A cotton farmer would grow vegetables and keep hogs and chickens, for example, for his family to eat and also to feed the Africans he kept. Often he would train some of his African laborers to be shoemakers, blacksmiths, carpenters, and tailors. The most successful plantations could supply most of their own needs.

The planters were hard-working people. They grew wealthy by producing large crops with as little cost to themselves as possible. In most of the Southern states cotton was the most important crop. Southerners understood the importance of cotton to their area, and knew that what affected the market for cotton affected all aspects of their lives. They also understood the importance of African labor for tending the cotton fields.

Negroes for Sale.

A Cargo of very fine stout Men and Women, in good order and fit for immediate service, just imported from the Windward Coast of Africa, in the Ship Two Brothers.—

Conditions are one half Cash or Produce, the other half payable the first of January next, giving Bond and Security if required.

The Sale to be opened at 10 o'Clock each Day, in Mr. Bourdeaux's Yard, at No. 48, on the Bay.

May 19, 1784. JOHN MITCHELL.

Thirty Seasoned Negroes

To be Sold for Credit, at Private Sale.

AMONGST which is a Carpenter, none of whom are known to be dishonest.

Also, to be sold for Cash, a regular bred young Negroe Man-Cook, born in this Country, who served several Years under an exceeding good French Cook abroad, and his Wife a middle aged Washer-Woman, (both very honest) and their two Children. *Likewise,* a young Man a Carpenter.

For Terms apply to the Printer.

With the wealth produced by the blossoming agriculture came the idea of the cavalier South. The large planters wanted to think of themselves as cavaliers, or gentlemen, dedicated to a way of life where politeness and courtesy were all-important and where honor held a higher place than the desire to make money. Southerners referred to the African captives, at least in public, as their "servants," and often complained about the burden of caring for them.

These planters were a minority in the South, but like wealthy minorities at any time, they had a great deal of political power. By banding together, they protected their interests and the way of life that allowed them to thrive.

Smaller planters competed as best they could against their larger neighbors. While large planters usually had overseers to manage the field hands, small planters often worked with their Africans. Large plantation owners sometimes held hundreds of Africans. Small farmers might hold two or three, or none at all. As land became more expensive, it was the small planter who suffered most.

Poor whites suffered under the plantation system. The South was chiefly agricultural, and the workers used in that area were African captives; poor whites could not compete in the job market with free labor. There was little industry in the South. Hinton R. Helper, a critic of the Southern economy, would later remark that a Southern man spent most of his life trying to

Early advertisements for Africans. The first is for Africans newly captured, the other for Africans born in America, detailing their skills. *Library of Congress* raise cotton for Northern mills; he would die and be buried in a suit made in the North, have a passage read from a Bible printed in the North, and be laid to rest in a grave dug with a Yankee spade. Many poor whites who wanted to be carpenters or builders, or pursue other trades, often found themselves competing with the Africans. Even jobs away from the plantations were often filled by Africans, with the payment for their labor being turned over to the owners. Many poor whites supplemented their living by becoming "patrollers," guarding the plantation areas to keep the Africans from escaping.

How the Africans were treated varied from plantation to plantation. Some were treated harshly with beatings and back-breaking work. Others were treated more humanely, and were never in great physical distress.

Africans knew they were valuable to the plantation owner and could sometimes use that value to their advantage. When an owner was particularly harsh, he would often find that his captives worked a lot slower, producing less profit for him.

The African was valuable to the plantation owner both as a worker and as an asset that could be sold or mortgaged. Often plantation owners who needed money would borrow against the value of the Africans they held. In that evolved value there existed a relationship and an interdependency that did not exist between any other people in the country.

Under the plantation system the new colonies of North America offered, to the white man willing to work hard and use African labor, the chance to become wealthy. Nowhere else in the world was this chance as clear; nowhere else in the world could the ordinary person find this opportunity.

The staple crops that the system produced were in demand all over the world. During the colonial period much of the wealth of North America was generated under the plantation system. Without the plantation wealth of Virginia, Georgia, and the Carolinas, the colonies might never have sought their independence from England.

4

To Make a Slave

We have seen that the colonists needed labor to build their fortunes and, in the process, build a nation. And we have seen their willingness to take that labor, by force, from Africans. But African men and women did not willingly surrender their lives. The people who came from the boats were Africans, captured by a strange tribe. The plantation owners did not want captives longing for freedom, looking for ways to overthrow those who held them; they wanted slaves, people who would work without having to be constantly watched, who would grow to believe that their oppression was somehow right. The owners called the process of changing, or attempting to change, captives into slaves "seasoning."

The dominant instrument in this process was the gun. Guns, and the threat of instant death, forced the African to obey the be loaded with Africans and how long the voyage from Africa took. It was not unusual for 10 percent of the Africans to die if the trip took longer than the usual twenty-five to thirty-five days.

Ibrahima, now twenty-six years old, reached Mississippi in 1788. As the ship approached land, the Africans were brought onto the deck and fed. Some had oil put on their skins so they would look better; their sores were treated or covered with pitch. Then they were given garments to wear in an obvious effort to improve their appearance.

Although Ibrahima could not speak English, he understood he was being bargained for. The white man who stood on the platform with him made him turn around, and several other white men neared him, touched his limbs, examined his teeth, looked into his eyes, and made him move about.

Thomas Foster, a tobacco grower and a hard-working man, had come from South Carolina with his family and had settled on the rich lands that took their minerals from the Mississippi River. He already held one captive, a young boy. In August 1788 he bought two more. One of them was named Sambo, which means "second son." The other was Ibrahima.

Foster agreed to pay $930 for the two Africans. He paid $150 down and signed an agreement to pay another $250 the following January and the remaining $530 in January of the following year.

When Ibrahima arrived at Foster's farm, he tried to find someone who could explain to the white man who he was—the will of the master. The whippings and other punishments were effective only when it was very clear that fighting back was impossible. The owners tried to convince the Africans that they were helpless. Most whites in the South carried guns. Overseers would sometimes take the Africans with them when they hunted to demonstrate the power of the gun.

But it was obvious that an even more extensive system would have to be created if large numbers of Africans were going to be held for years. The patrol system was part of the answer. Whites on horseback patrolled the roads and areas in which Africans were held, stopping any Africans they found away from the plantations and demanding proof that the Africans had permission to be away from the fields or quarters. Those Africans who could not provide proof were beaten and taken back to their masters. Here is how one former captive described it:

Yes, they had church meetings. People used to go from house to house. Old Harry Brown, he was a kind of preacher. He used to preach to us right smart. 'Cause they had to watch for the paddyrollers [patrollers]. They generally come in twos and threes. They come twixt eight and twelve at night. If they catch you having meetings, they'd arrest you. Yes sir! They had bloodhounds with them. 'Twarnt no way in the world you could get away. No sir! They didn't have the same men on the patrols all the time. Different men every night.

from *Weevils in the Wheat: Interviews with Ex-Slaves*
by Archie Booker

The patrol system was important enough to be written into state laws.

Sec. 983. All white male owners of slaves, below the age of sixty years, and all other free white persons, between the ages of eighteen and forty-five years, who are not disabled by sickness or bodily infirmity, except commissioned officers in the militia, and persons exempt by law from the performance of militia duty, are subject to perform patrol duty.

from *The Code of Alabama, 1852*

But the network of owners and patrols was not enough. The owners still had to find a way to exercise complete control over the Africans. What they needed was to change the way the Africans thought of themselves.

The Africans brought to North America knew who they were. They were Mandingo, or Fula, or Hausa, Yoruba, or Bambara. They knew they were Africans and knew they were the captives of the people who held them.

The plantation owners wanted to change the Africans into some new thing. Agricultural magazines such as *Southern Cultivator*, *Farmers' Register*, *Carolina Planter*, and *South-Western Farmer* ran articles on the "management of Negroes." One way was through the use of religion, which instructed the Africans to obey their masters.

The great duty, then, to be performed is—not to convince the Mississippians of the importance of instructing their slaves in the principles of religion—but to point out the best methods. Here, happily, we are not left in the dark to grope our way with untried theories—for many planters, both in this state and Louisiana, have long been pursuing a systematic plan in this matter, and, as we are happy to hear, with the most pleasing results. Indeed, so far back as 1835 . . . measures were in extensive progress among many of our plantations, which bade fair to produce highly beneficial effects upon our black population.

from *South-Western Farmer*, February 3, 1843

Symbols of African heritage were systematically removed. Long hair was cut, African religious rituals were forbidden, and individuals were separated from others who spoke their language. The dietary needs of Africans who were Islamic were ignored. They were given western names, often names the owner found amusing or that mocked the captives' status. Ibrahima was called "Prince" by Thomas Foster. Other Africans were called "Caesar" or "Plato." They were called "niggers" or "Negroes." Neither name carried an African history or tradition. The owners broke down the captives' African identity and substituted one the owners themselves had invented. The captives responded by disguising their African ways. The music they sang was African in form, but the words were English. Thus was born the spiritual.

Family structures among Africans were very formal, but most owners disregarded the family unit. Some owners did allow their captives to marry, but the marriage was only a formality. It was still the owner who controlled the captives' families and who had authority over their children. The idea that a man *could* be sold away from his wife, or that a child *could* be sold away from its mother, diminished the value of marriage and family. The captives lost their identities as parents, husbands, or wives. The Africans responded by changing the definition of the family. Any child, any person, could be accepted into any

N. B. FOREST,
DEALER IN SLAVES,
No. 87 Adams-st, Memphis, Ten.,

HAS just received from North Carolina, twenty-five likely young negroes, to which he desires to call the attention of purchasers. He will be in the regular receipt of negroes from North and South Carolina every month. His Negro Depot is one of the most complete and commodious establishments of the kind in the Southern country, and his regulations exact and systematic, cleanliness, neatness and comfort being strictly observed and enforced. His aim is to furnish to customers A. 1 servants' and field hands, sound and perfect in body and mind. Negroes taken on commission.   Jan21

Memphis slave dealer Nathan Bedford Forrest became an outstanding Confederate general and one of the founders of the Ku Klux Klan. *The Bettmann Archive*

intact family. The Africans created the extended family.

Ignorance was another tool used in the battle to turn the captives into slaves. When it was discovered how easily the Africans learned, and how eager they were to do so, laws were created forbidding anyone to teach an African to read.

"On Sundays," relates a woman once held in bondage, "I have seen the Negroes up in the country going away under large oaks, and in secret places, sitting in the woods with spelling books."

Charity Bower, interviewed by Lydia Maria Child, 1848

Africans understood that being able to read gave them abilities that the owners did not want them to have, but they took the chance of being punished as they read by candlelight at night or took whatever books they could find into the forests. The planters certainly did not want the Africans thinking about ideas of freedom and equality, ideas that their own sons and daughters were exploring in school. They didn't want them to read newspaper articles about the debates in Congress over the expansion of slavery, or to realize how many white Americans thought Africans should be free. Nor did they want them to read about other Africans who were free in Northern states, or who had escaped to Canada.

It's difficult to tell just how many Africans were brought into North America, for few accurate records remain. Most historians believe that somewhere between 250,000 and 400,000 men, women, and children were taken from Africa and brought to North America between 1620 and 1808. This does not include the thousands who died on the ships or those killed during the kidnaping process. No records were kept of the thousands of Africans illegally brought to North America after 1808. When the ships carrying Africans could not outrun the navy ships that challenged them, they tried to destroy the evidence by simply throwing their human cargo overboard. It is estimated that only 10 percent of all the African captives were brought to the area that became the United States. The rest were taken to the Caribbean and South America.

Eventually, most of those who were held captive had been

born in what had become the United States. An effort was made by the owners to make these descendants feel inferior because of their African heritage; the fact that they had been deprived of direct knowledge of that heritage made it easier, and soon the smallest African children were taught to treat all white children as their masters.

Most of all there was an attempt to make the African feel both inferior to his owner and dependent on him.

The Negro should feel that his master is lawgiver and judge, and yet is his protector and friend but so far above him as never to be approached save in the most respectful manner.

"Management of Negroes," *Southern Cultivator*, June 1851

Some of the African captives, assuming the feelings of inferiority that the masters sought, went even further. They adopted the attitude that anything associated with their African past was inferior as well. To them, dark skin color and African facial features or hair were "bad." Those who adopted these notions were, of course, treated better by their masters.

Many Africans resisted the attempts to give them a "slave" mentality by doing anything they could to be free. Others resisted in more subtle ways. They couldn't refuse to do the master's bidding for fear of beatings or of being sold, but they could—and did—pretend that they had great difficulty learning tasks.

The Africans adapted many beliefs common to their African heritage to their newly adopted religion of Christianity. Spiritual possession, while common in Africa, was not part of the European religious experience. It did become part of the African experience and was widely practiced, especially in the Pentecostal church. Combining religion with daily life served as not only a reminder of their African heritage but was a source of strength for the soul in bondage. Plantation owners watching African religious services were often impressed with their apparent happiness at the prospect of a less painful afterlife. What they did not realize was that the Africans were not so much looking forward to the prospect of a distant heaven, but rather celebrating the sanctity of the moments they were then and there creating in fellowship with other Africans, a fellowship the plantation owners would doubtlessly have found dangerous if they had understood it.

While secretly learning to read and write the language of their owners, they passed their own words and customs from generation to generation and created new customs that identified them as a people. Within the yoke of their captivity they began the battle for freedom and dignity.

5

The United States of America!

Nations are created in many ways, but usually throughout history one group or tribe of people defeats its enemies and declares a section of land its own. Great Britain had extended its nation this way by establishing eighteen colonies in North America after defeating the Native Americans who had lived in the eastern part of the continent. But the thirteen lower colonies were growing restive under British rule. There was talk among the colonists of starting a new nation. The very idea of a new nation, formed by men of intelligence and free from the defects so apparent in other nations, was wildly exciting. Ideas were being discussed in parlors and taverns about the country—ideas like equality and freedom. If a new country was formed, it would be the best opportunity the world had ever seen to put those ideas into effect.

The New England colonies were prospering in shipbuilding and a growing industrial trade. The great northern cities of New York and Philadelphia were bustling with people, and there was an excitement in the air. These "Americans," as many colonists were fond of calling themselves, were a new kind of people, experiencing freedoms they had never known in Europe—freedom of religion, freedom to travel, and freedom of speech. Many had traveled to the New World for just these opportunities.

The English colonists realized their power. And they also realized that their interests were not the same as those of England. The Spanish colonies had looser ties with Spain, as did the French with France. But it was Great Britain that had the most control in North America. And it was this control that was bothersome to the colonists.

In 1775 the united colonies decided to take up arms against the British. The following year they formally declared their independence and prepared to defend it with their lives.

Thomas Jefferson was a Virginian, a gentleman, and a statesman. It was he who drew up the Declaration of Independence. In his early draft he said that it was necessary for the colonies to break away from Great Britain. But he also accused the English king of participating in the slave trade.

[H]e has waged cruel war against human nature itself, violating it's [sic] most sacred rights of life & liberty in the persons of a distant people who never offended him, captivating & carrying them into slavery in another hemisphere or to incur miserable death in their transportation thither.

+ Dr. Franklin

valuable
abolishing our most important & valuable Laws

for taking away our charters & altering fundamentally the forms of our governments;
for suspending our own legislatures & declaring themselves invested with power to
legislate for us in all cases whatsoever:
he has abdicated government here, [by declaring us out of his protection & waging war against us.
withdrawing his governors, & declaring us out
of his allegiance & protection;]

he has plundered our seas, ravaged our coasts, burnt our towns & destroyed the
lives of our people:

Scotch and other
he is at this time transporting large armies of foreign mercenaries to compleat
the works of death, desolation & tyranny, already begun with circumstances
scarcely paralleled in the most barbarous ages, and totally
of cruelty & perfidy unworthy the head of a civilized nation:
he has endeavored to bring on the inhabitants of our frontiers the merciless Indian
savages, whose known rule of warfare is an undistinguished destruction of
all ages, sexes, & conditions [of existence:]

[he has incited treasonable insurrections of our fellow citizens, with the
allurements of forfeiture & confiscation of our property.
he has constrained others
he has waged cruel war against human nature itself, violating it's most sa-
-cred rights of life & liberty in the persons of a distant people who never of-
-fended him, captivating & carrying them into slavery in another hemi-
-sphere, or to incur miserable death in their transportation thither. this
piratical warfare, the opprobrium of infidel powers, is the warfare of the
Christian king of Great Britain. determined to keep open a market
where MEN should be bought & sold, he has prostituted his negative
for suppressing every legislative attempt to prohibit or to restrain this
determining to keep open a market where MEN should be bought & should:
execrable commerce: and that this assemblage of horrors might want no fact
of distinguished die, he is now exciting those very people to rise in arms
among us, and to purchase that liberty of which he has deprived them,
by murdering the people upon whom he also obtruded them: thus paying
off former crimes committed against the liberties of one people, with crimes
which he urges them to commit against the lives of another.]

in every stage of these oppressions we have petitioned for redress in the most humble
only
terms; our repeated petitions have been answered by repeated injuries. a prince
whose character is thus marked by every act which may define a tyrant, is unfit
free
to be the ruler of a people who mean to be free. future ages will scarce believe
that the hardiness of one man adventured within the short compass of twelve years
to build a foundation so broad & undisguised, for tyranny
only, over a people fostered & fixed in principles
of freedom.]

+ Dr. Franklin

Here Jefferson is condemning the slave trade. But colonists in New England were engaged in the slave trade, and Africans who "never offended" Americans were being bought and sold every day. And colonists from the South were certainly using slave labor.

A new version of the Declaration of Independence was drawn up, omitting the reference to the slave trade.

The colonists were declaring their right to "Life, Liberty, and the Pursuit of Happiness." But what about the Africans who were being held throughout the colonies? What about the Africans who were being held by Thomas Jefferson? How could a man who loved liberty, who was willing to lay down his life for liberty, still hold others in captivity? Clearly the Declaration of Independence, so precious to so many, was avoiding dealing with the issue of the rights of Africans being held in bondage.

Jefferson recognized this dilemma and spent much time wrestling with both the moral and intellectual aspects of it. He finally came to the conclusion that while the continued importation of captives was wrong, the more urgent problem was how to deal with the Africans who were already living in North America.

The new country—or rather, the country that wanted to be new—chose a commander-in-chief of its Army—George Washington. The forty-five-year-old Washington was born in 1732,

An early draft of the Declaration of Independence. Jefferson's objections to the English slave trade were deleted in the final version. *Library of Congress*

George Washington on his Virginia plantation. *Library of Congress*

and had led colonial troops in the French and Indian Wars. As a young man he had studied surveying and had inherited both land and Africans from his father. He was interested in the business of planting and was known for his careful attention to detail.

As a young man Washington cut a dashing figure. He was quite tall, with an athletic build. Perhaps it was his early reputation as a horseman and gentleman, or his love for dancing, that attracted the lovely widow of Daniel Parke Custis.

Martha Dandridge, born in 1731, was the daughter of John Dandridge, who had come to America in 1711 with his older brother. Martha had married Daniel Parke Custis when she was eighteen. The Custis family was one of the wealthiest in Virginia, and when Custis died, the young, attractive widow was considered a good catch. Colonel George Washington was

Martha, one of the first Dandridges born in America. When she married the young George Washington, she brought with her the more than three hundred Africans she had held from her previous marriage. *Library of Congress*

twenty-six when he met Martha, and the handsome couple was soon married.

Before his marriage, Washington had not been a wealthy man. Martha, who had inherited her first husband's money, lands, and Africans, changed that. When Washington's brother Lawrence died in 1761, George also inherited the large estate in Virginia called Mount Vernon. It was here that the Washingtons lived, using many of the Africans as house and personal "servants," as was the custom.

Washington, a Virginian by birth, represented a study in contrasts typical of his time. On the one hand he considered slavery an evil practice and against the best interests of the country. On the other hand there were over three hundred Africans on his plantations.

The War of Independence found a ragtag American army, poorly equipped and poorly supported by the new government, fighting against a much better trained British army. But while the American army was poorly equipped, the British army was vastly overconfident.

The Revolutionary War dragged on from 1775 until 1781 before the British decided they had had enough. They had fought a war to which they never seemed completely committed. They had tried to enlist the help of Native Americans and were partially successful, and had entertained the possibility of arming the thousands of Africans held by the colonists. But they

Lord Dunmore's proclamation offering freedom to "indented" servants and Negroes willing to fight for Great Britain. *Library of Congress*

By his Excellency the Right Honourable JOHN Earl of DUNMORE, his

Majesty's Lieutenant and Governor-General of the Colony and Dominion of

Virginia, and Vice-Admiral of the same:

A PROCLAMATION.

AS I have ever entertained Hopes that an Accommodation might have taken Place between *Great Britain* and this Colony, without being compelled, by my Duty, to this most disagreeable, but now absolutely necessary Step, rendered so by a Body of armed Men, unlawfully assembled, firing on his Majesty's Tenders, and the Formation of an Army, and that Army now on their March to attack his Majesty's Troops, and destroy the well-disposed Subjects of this Colony: To defeat such treasonable Purposes, and that all such Traitors, and their Abetters, may be brought to Justice, and that the Peace and good Order of this Colony may be again restored, which the ordinary Course of the civil Law is unable to effect, I have thought fit to issue this my Proclamation, hereby declaring, that until the aforesaid good Purposes can be obtained, I do, in Virtue of the Power and Authority to me given, by his Majesty, determine to execute martial Law, and cause the same to be executed throughout this Colony; and to the End that Peace and good Order may the sooner be restored, I do require every Person capable of bearing Arms to resort to his Majesty's STAN-DARD, or be looked upon as Traitors to his Majesty's Crown and Government, and thereby become liable to the Penalty the Law inflicts upon such Offences, such as Forfeiture of Life, Confiscation of Lands, &c. &c. And I do hereby farther declare all indented Servants, Negroes, or others (appertaining to Rebels) free, that are able and willing to bear Arms, they joining his Majesty's Troops, as soon as may be, for the more speedily reducing this Colony to a proper Sense of their Duty, to his Majesty's Crown and Dignity. I do farther order, and require, all his Majesty's liege Subjects to retain their Quitrents, or any other Taxes due, or that may become due, in their own Custody, till such Time as Peace may be again restored to this at present most unhappy Country, or demanded of them for their former salutary Purposes, by Officers properly authorised to receive the same.

GIVEN under my Hand, on Board the Ship William, off Norfolk,

the 7th Day of November, in the 16th Year of his Majesty's Reign.

DUNMORE.

GOD SAVE THE KING.

were uneasy with this idea. Although a proclamation by Lord Dunmore offered freedom to Africans who would fight with them, when they captured Africans who had fought against the British, they often sold them in the West Indies.

What *did* the Revolutionary War mean to Africans? Many Africans were to fight side by side with the colonists, only to be returned to bondage after the war. Others were freed because of their valiant service.

It was the prosperity of the colonies that gave the revolutionaries the resources to break off from England. To a large extent, the colonies' wealth was created by the labor of the Africans.

By the time of the Revolutionary War, not all Africans on American soil were enslaved. Some had managed to obtain their own freedom, and of these, some fought for the revolutionists against England.

6

James Forten

Not all Africans were being held on plantations. Some had bought their own freedom; others had been given it by the whites who held them. And when the Africans became free, they did what other Americans were doing. Some worked their own farms; many worked on ships; others started their own business ventures. In Ellicott Mills, Maryland, a free African man named Benjamin Banneker began publishing his almanac and corresponded with Thomas Jefferson. In New York a free African named Samuel Fraunces owned a famous tavern in which George Washington as well as all the leading New Yorkers would eat. An escaped African, Crispus Attucks, was one of five protesters killed when the British fired on a group of colonists in Boston. Hundreds of Africans joined the fight against the British as sailors and soldiers. One of those was James Forten.

Philadelphia harbor in 1778. James Forten lived nearby. *Courtesy, The Henry Francis du Pont Winterthur Museum*

It was early morning on Tuesday, September 2, 1766, in the city of Philadelphia. The roads into the city were already filling with farmers bringing in produce to sell. Windows in the city were coming alive with the glow of lamplight. Small factory owners trudged through the winding streets to small shops. Printers, shoemakers, blacksmiths, candle makers, bakers—all began the business of the day. For Philadelphia was indeed a city of business.

54

As day broke over the harbor, the masts of the ships loomed against the gray skies. The ships rocked at their moorings as if they, too, were ready for the new day.

Hundreds of free men of African descent lived in Philadelphia. The city was the home of a number of noted abolitionists—people who wanted to abolish, or do away with, the practice of slavery—including the Quakers, a powerful and influential religious group. More important was the fact that Africans could find work in Philadelphia.

Many of the Africans worked the docks, loading and unloading the ships that brought products to the colonies from all over the world. Others were tradesmen and seamstresses, cooks, barbers, and common laborers. All along the eastern seaboard, from Baltimore to New England, free Africans worked on boats, hauling loads, carrying passengers, and fishing. Many opened restaurants. Others bought their own boats and tried their luck on the brisk waterfronts.

Thomas Forten, a free African, was employed by Robert Bridges, a sailmaker in Philadelphia. Sail making was a profitable but difficult job. Sewing the coarse cloth was brutal on the hands. The heavy thread had to be waxed and handled with dexterity. A person trying to break the thread with his hands could see it cut through his flesh like a knife. But Forten appreciated his job. It paid reasonably well and the work was steady.

Forten helped in all aspects of sail making and assisted in installing the sails on the ships the firm serviced. With the income from his work he had purchased his wife's freedom.

Now, on this early Tuesday morning, a new baby was due. The baby, born later that day, was James Forten.

Young James Forten's early life was not that different from that of other poor children living in Philadelphia. He played marbles and blindman's buff, and he raced in the streets. When he was old enough, he would go down to the docks to see the ships.

Sometimes James went to the shop where his father worked and did odd jobs. Bridges liked him and let him work as much as he could, but he also encouraged Thomas Forten to make sure that his son learned to read and write.

The Fortens sent their son to the small school that had been created for African children by a Quaker, Anthony Benezet. He believed that the only way the Africans would ever take a meaningful place in the colonies would be through education.

Thomas Forten was working on a ship when he fell to his death. James Forten was only seven at the time. His mother was devastated, but still insisted that her son continue school. He did so for two more years, after which he took a job working in a small store.

What James wanted to do was to go to sea. He was fourteen in 1781 when his mother finally relented and gave her permission. America was fighting for its freedom, and James Forten would be fighting, too.

He knew about the difficulties between the British and the American colonists. He had seen first British soldiers and then American soldiers marching through the streets of Philadelphia. Among the American soldiers were men of color.

A black child in Philadelphia in the 1700's had to be careful. There were stories of free Africans being kidnaped and sold into slavery. He had seen the captives on the ships. They looked like him: the same dark skin, the same wide nose; but there was a sadness about them that both touched his heart and frightened him. He had seen Africans in chains being marched through the streets, on their way to the South. He never forgot the sight of his people in bondage, or accepted it as natural that black people should be slaves.

But the black soldiers Forten saw were something special. Marching with muskets on their shoulders, they seemed taller and blacker than any men he had ever seen. And there were African sailors, too. He knew some of these men. They had been fishermen and haulers before the conflict with Great Britain; now they worked on privateers and navy ships. Sometimes he heard talk about naval battles, and he tried to imagine what they must have been like.

In the summer of 1781, James Forten signed onto the privateer *Royal Louis*, commanded by Stephen Decatur, Sr. The colonies had few ships of their own to fight against the powerful British navy and issued "letters of marque" to private parties. These allowed the ships, under the flag of the United States, to attack British ships and to profit from the sale of any vessel captured.

The *Royal Louis* sailed out of Philadelphia in August and was quickly engaged by the British vessel *Active*, a heavily armed brig sent from England to protect its trade ships.

The *Royal Louis*'s guns were loaded with gunpowder that was tamped down by an assistant gunner. Then the cannonball was put into the barrel and pushed against the powder. Then the powder would be ignited. The powder had to be kept belowdecks in case of a hit by an enemy ship. "Powder monkeys," usually young boys between ten and fifteen, carried the powder from below to the guns.

Forten was a powder monkey. Up and down the stairs he raced with the powder as shots from the British ship whistled overhead. There were large holes in the sails and men screaming as they were hit with grapeshot that splintered the sides of the ship. The smell of gunpowder filled the air as Captain Decatur turned his ship to keep his broadside guns trained on the *Active*. Sailors all about Forten were falling, some dying even as others cried for more powder.

Again he went belowdecks, knowing that if a shot ripped through to the powder kegs, or if any of the burning planks fell down into the hold, he would be killed instantly in the explosion. Up he came again with as much powder as he could carry.

After what must have seemed forever with the two ships tacking about each other like angry cats, the *Active* lowered its flag. It had surrendered!

Decatur brought his ship into Philadelphia, its guns still trained on the limping *Active*.

The crowd on the dock cheered wildly as they recognized the American flag on the *Royal Louis*. On board the victorious ship James Forten had mixed feelings as he saw so many of his comrades wounded, some mortally.

The *Royal Louis* turned its prisoners over to military authorities. On the 27th of September, the *Active* was sold; the proceeds were split among the owners of the *Royal Louis* and the crew.

The sailors with the worst wounds were sent off to be cared for. The others, their own wounds treated, were soon about the business of repairing the ship. Forten must have been excited. Once the fear of the battle had subsided and the wounded were taken off, it was easy to think about the dangerous encounter in terms of adventure. And they had won.

The missing crew was replaced. The ship was checked carefully by its captain and found to be in fine fighting condition. The crew carried more ammunition aboard, more powder, and fresh provisions. Once more they sailed for open waters.

On the 16th of October, 1781, they sighted a ship, recognized it as British, and made for it instantly. As they neared, a second ship was spotted, and then a third. Decatur turned to escape the trap, but it was already too late. The three British ships, the *Amphyon*, the *Nymph*, and the sloop *Pomona*, closed in. It was soon clear that the *Royal Louis* had two choices: to surrender or to be sunk.

The *Royal Louis* lowered its flag. It had surrendered, and its crew were now prisoners. Forten was terrified. He had heard the stories of the British sending captured Africans to the West Indies to be sold into slavery. He knew the *Pomona* had sailed back and forth from the colonies to the island of Barbados, where many Africans already languished in bondage. It was a time for dread.

James was taken aboard the *Amphyon* with others from his crew. On board the British ship Captain Beasley inspected the

59

prisoners. There were several boys among the American crew, and he separated them from the older men.

Captain Beasley's son looked over the boys who had been captured. Many of them were younger than he was. Although still prisoners, the boys were given more freedom than the men, and Beasley's son saw the Americans playing marbles. He joined in the game, and it was during this playing that he befriended Forten.

The result of this tentative friendship was that Captain Beasley did not, as he might have done, send Forten to a ship bound for the West Indies and slavery. Instead he was treated as a regular prisoner of war and sent to the prison ship the *Jersey*.

Dark and forbidding, the *Jersey* was a sixty-gunner anchored off Long Island, in New York. It had been too old to use in the war and had been refitted first as a hospital ship and then as a ship for prisoners. The portholes had been sealed and twenty-inch squares carved into her sides. Across these squares iron bars were placed.

The captain of the *Jersey* greeted the prisoners with a sneer. All were searched under the watchful eyes of British marines. The wounded were unattended, the sick ignored. The pitiful cries of other prisoners came from belowdecks. A few pale, sickly prisoners, covered with sores, were huddled around a water cask. Then came the cry that some would hear for months, others for years.

"Down, Rebels, down!"

They were rebels against the king, to be despised, perhaps to be hanged. Traitors, they were being called, not soldiers of

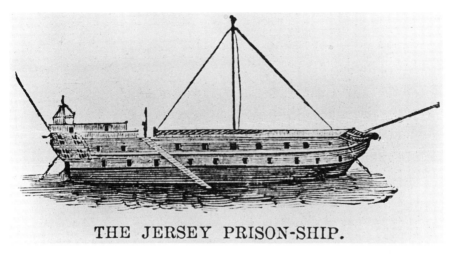

THE JERSEY PRISON-SHIP.

Many an American sailor languished on the notorious British prison ship *Jersey*, which was docked off Long Island, New York. *New York Public Library, Schomburg Collection*

America. James was pushed into a line on deck. The line shuffled toward the water cask, where each man could fill a canteen with a pint of water. Then they were pushed roughly below-decks.

The hold of the ship was dark. What little light there was came from the small squares along the hull. The air was dank as men relieved themselves where they lay. Some of the prisoners were moaning. Others manned pumps to remove the water from the bottom of the boat.

Sleep was hard coming, and James wasn't sure if he wouldn't still be sold into slavery. Beasley's son had liked him, he remembered, and the boy had offered to persuade his father to take James to England. It would have been better than the hold of the *Jersey*.

In the morning the first thing the crew did was to check to see how many prisoners had died during the night. Many of the prisoners were sick with yellow fever. For these death would be just a matter of time.

Forten later claimed that the game of marbles with Beasley's son had saved him from a life of slavery in the West Indies. But on November 1, two weeks after the capture of the *Royal Louis*, the news reached New York that Brigadier General Charles Cornwallis, commander of the British army in Virginia, had surrendered to George Washington. Washington had strongly protested the British practice of sending prisoners to the West Indies. It was probably the news of his victory, more than the game of marbles, that saved the young sailor.

James Forten was not a hero. He did not singlehandedly defeat the British, or sink a ship. But he fought, like so many other Africans, for the freedom of America, and he fought well. He was only one of thousands of Africans who helped to create the country known as the United States of America.

In Philadelphia, after the war, James Forten became an apprentice to the man his father had worked for, Robert Bridges. Like his father, James was a hard worker. Eventually he would run the business for Robert Bridges, and by 1798 he owned it. At its height the business employed forty workers, both black and white. Forten became one of the wealthiest men in Philadelphia. He married and raised a family, passing on to them the values of hard work he had learned from his father. Forten made several major contributions to the sail-making business, among them a method of handling the huge sails in a shop, which allowed sails to be repaired much faster and saved precious time for shipowners. In the coming years he would use his great wealth to support both antislavery groups and the right of women to vote—at a time when over 90 percent of all Africans in America were still in a state of enslavement.

James Forten became one of the most influential of the African abolitionists. He spent much of his life pleading for the freedom of his people in the country his people had helped to create.

7

We the People . . .

Philadelphia was the home of James Forten, and of a large community of free Africans. Many of them gathered around the town square and listened to the talk of the new government that was being formed. Shopkeepers debated whether or not the United States of America should have a king. Visitors from New Jersey were delighted that they would have as many senators as the largest states. Some of the gentlemen from Delaware weren't sure if they wanted to join the union or not. But for the Africans the problems of balancing the interests of small and large states, of deciding who could declare war, were not nearly as important as the question of whether or not people of African descent would be free.

How could anyone deny that Africans had fought to free the country from British rule? How could anyone deny that a black man, Peter Salem, had killed the English Major John Pitcairn at the battle of Bunker Hill? A stir of excitement came with the announcement that a stated purpose of the Constitution was to "secure the blessings of liberty to ourselves and our posterity."

Inside the meeting hall none of the delegates seemed to have the enthusiasm for creating a nation that they had displayed before and during the war. Wise old Benjamin Franklin, in failing health, guessed that they were playing it close to the vest, each working for his own form of government, for his own interests. James Madison from Virginia was taking a leading role in the debates; he was worried about the banking system.

The Africans in Philadelphia noted that some of the Southern delegates had brought with them blacks whom they held on southern plantations as personal "servants."

It became clear to the Africans that the Southern delegates were very influential and regarded themselves as a group distinct from the rest of the country. It was also clear that putting together a constitution that would satisfy all the states would not be easy. As the delegates within the hall hammered out the points of the Constitution, the Africans outside tried to figure out what each phrase and article would mean to them.

There were many issues to be considered. Some were relatively easy to deal with, and others disturbed the delegates to the point of threatening the very existence of the fledgling nation. What they wanted to do was to proclaim the existence of a great nation—a great nation and a great people who would embrace freedom and democracy as never before. But how could they do this while slavery still existed?

Some of the Northern delegates wanted to discuss the morality of slavery, thinking they could offer compelling reasons for the country to abolish the practice. Other delegates were worried about the security of the nation. They recalled that Lord Dunmore's proclamation promised freedom to any African who joined the British cause. If the British had armed the Africans and had promised them freedom without reservation, the result of the war might have been quite different. Holding within a country a large group of people who had ample reason to turn against it was a distinct danger. There was no mistaking that the interests of the many Africans held captive on Southern plantations were not represented by the influential men who attended the Constitutional Convention.

Southern delegates pointed out that it was New Englanders who had first transported Africans into the colonies and who were the first to participate and profit from the slave trade. The Northern mills that used the cheap cotton produced by the South also profited from the labor of the Africans. But it was John Rutledge of South Carolina who framed the issue most clearly when he said that interest alone is the governing principle of nations.

In other words, each section of the country would define its own interests and try to promote them.

The question at hand, the Southern states declared, was not whether or not slavery was moral, profitable to the nation, or justified, but whether the Southern states, which held slaves, would join the union at all.

The delegates decided in 1787 that it was more important to

form a nation than to end slavery. And it was to this end that the framers of the Constitution worked.

In the South the men who owned the plantations ran the states. Influential on all levels of government, they exercised their will at the convention. What was good for the planters, they maintained, was good for the South.

This idea—that a relatively few plantation owners could decide what was best for all the people without the representation of those people's wishes—was the same idea that the colonists had rebelled against during the Revolutionary War (No taxation without representation!). Nevertheless, the large Southern planters became, in effect, a ruling aristocracy.

There were also many statesmen, in both the North and the South, who wanted to do away with human bondage.

By the end of the convention, however, it was Rutledge who proved to be right. It was to the interests of the colonies to form a new country, and to keep the wealth and talent of the South as part of that country as well as the industry and talent of the North. And this was done.

The Constitution of the United States is a document designed to insure the freedom of the common person. It is also a document that balanced the powers of the large states and the small, and that prevented power from being centralized in a dictatorship. The delegates were proud of the Constitution they created, and of the democracy it celebrated. They decided not to deal with what now seems an obvious question: How could a nation that proclaimed the freedom of all people ignore the fact that many people within its borders were not free? In fact there are only three references to the existence of the Africans in the Constitution.

Article I, Section 2 said in part:

Representatives and direct taxes shall be apportioned among the several States which may be included within this Union, according to their respective numbers, which shall be determined by adding to the whole number of free persons, including those bound to service for a term of Years, and excluding Indians not taxed, *three-fifths of all other persons.* [Emphasis supplied.]

The "three-fifths of all other persons" referred to Africans held in bondage. Each state was allowed a certain number of representatives in the House of Representatives. The number of representatives, and therefore the number of votes each state had in the House, depended on the population of the state. Suppose each state was allowed five representatives for every one million people. If there were a million whites living in Virginia and a million Africans in bondage, the state would be allowed five representatives for the million whites and three for the Africans. (Of course the Africans would not receive the benefit of this representation.)

This was a concession to the Southern states, which feared the rapid population growth in the North and wanted more representation than would be afforded by a simple head count of free people.

The second reference to Africans was contained in Article I, Section 9, which says in part:

The migration or importation of such persons as any of the States now existing shall think proper to admit, shall not be prohibited by the Congress prior to the year one thousand eight hundred and eight, but a tax or duty may be imposed on such importation, not exceeding ten dollars for each person.

This was probably a concession to the North. It stated first that the trade in native Africans could not be stopped until 1808, and then that Congress could put a tax on the importation of Africans. Previously the Constitution referred to Africans as "all other persons," here it mentions the imported Africans in an equally roundabout way: "the migration or importation of *such persons . . .*"

The third reference to persons held in bondage was in Article IV, Section 2 of the Constitution:

No person held to service or labor in one State, under the laws thereof, escaping into another, shall in consequence of any law or regulation therein, be discharged from such service or labor, but shall be delivered up on claim of the party to whom such service or labor may be due.

The use of indentured servants had decreased considerably by 1776. "Persons held to service or labor" referred mainly to the Africans.

These Constitutional clauses, in effect, recognize the existence and legality of slavery without actually saying so.

In the Constitution's references to captive labor we can read many things. First, of course, is that it existed. Also, since the Constitution talks about securing the "blessings of liberty" for Americans and the Africans were not free, there was a question of whether the Africans were citizens of the United States.

For the African working in the fields, or for free people of African descent such as James Forten, the Constitution meant very little. Furthermore, the status of African captives was the same as it had been before the Constitutional Convention. Even Africans who had gained their freedom by fighting in the Revolutionary War—and many had—were not sure what it was that they had gained.

8

To Be a Slave

What was it like to be called a slave? What was it like to be "owned" by someone? There is no single answer to this question. There is the common experience of being considered inferior, of being bought and sold as if one were a horse or household furniture. Many people who sold Africans would often add a few household items to the sale so that they would not appear to be "slave dealers." Most plantation owners did not seem to realize that the Africans hated the very idea of not being free. (George Washington, in August of 1761, complained that his Africans ran away without cause.) But the best way to find out what it was like to spend a lifetime in bondage is to read the documents from those days.

Here, for example, is the account of Thomas B. Chaplin, himself a slaveholder in the state of South Carolina, concerning a trial in which he was on the jury. He is writing about the man who was on trial for killing an African he held in bondage.

[T]his demon in human shape, this pretended Christian member of the Baptist Church,—had this poor crippled negro—placed in an open out house—the wind blowing through a hundred cracks—his clothes wet to his waist—without a single blanket—& in freezing weather, with his back against a partition—shackles on his wrists, & chained to a bolt in the floor, and a chain around his neck—the chain passing through a partition behind him, & fastened on the other side—in this position this poor wretch was left for the night, a position that none but the most blood thirsty Tyrant could have placed a human being. My heart chills at the idea—and my blood boils at the base tyranny—The wretch returned to his victim the next morning—& found him, as any might expect, dead—choked—strangled frozen to death—murdered.

The death of the African was ruled an accident, and the man responsible for causing that death was allowed to go free.

For other Africans the experience was different. Consider the experience of Elias Thomas, from Raleigh, North Carolina.

We called the slave houses quarters. They were arranged like streets about two hundred yards on the north side of the great house.

Our food was pretty good. Our white folks used slaves, especially the children, as they did themselves about eating. We all had the same kind of food. All had plenty of clothes but only one pair of shoes a year. People went barefooted a lot then, more than they do now. We had good places to sleep, straw mattresses and chicken feather beds, and feather bolsters. A bolster reached clear across the head of the bed.

We worked from sun to sun, with one hour and a half to rest at noon or dinner time. I was so small I did not do much heavy work. I chopped

African children, like these from Louisiana, were not allowed to learn to read or write. They did light chores on the plantation until they were old enough to work in the fields. *Library of Congress*

corn and cotton mostly. The old slaves had patches they tended, and sold what they made and had the money it bought. Everybody ate out of the big garden, both white and black alike. Old Missus wouldn't allow us to eat rabbits, but she let us catch and eat possums. Missus didn't have any use for a rabbit. . . .

We thought well of the poor white neighbors. We colored children took them as regular playmates. Marster's boys played with them too, and Marster gave them all the work he could. He hired both men and women of the poor white class to work on the plantation. We all worked together. We had a good time. We worked and sang together and everybody seemed happy. In harvest time, a lot of help was hired, and such laughing, working, and singing. Just a good time in general. We sang the songs "Crossing over Jordan," and "Bound for the Promised Land."

Neither the extreme cruelty described by Chaplin nor the "good time" of Elias Thomas can be considered the essence of African captivity. That the cruelty *did* exist was one aspect of it. The cruelty did not have to be physical.

Consider the crushing heartbreak expressed in this letter of Maria Perkins to her husband, Richard. Probably Maria had someone write the letter for her, and Richard would have had someone read it to him if he received it.

Charlottesville, Oct. 8th, 1852

Dear Husband I write you a letter to let you know my distress   my master has sold albert to a trader on Monday court day and myself and other child is for sale also and I want you to let [me] hear from you very soon before next cort if you can I don't know when   I don't want you to wait till Chrismas   I want you to tell dr Hamelton and your master if either will buy me they can attend to it know and then I can go afterwards. I don't want a trader to get me   they asked me if I had got any person to buy me and I told them no   they took me to the court houste too   they never put me up a man buy the name of brady bought albert and is gone   I don't know where   they say he lives in Scottesvile   my things is in several places some is in staunton and if I should be sold I don't know what will become of them   I don't expect to meet with the luck to get that way till I am quite heartsick—nothing more—I am and ever will be your kind wife

Maria Perkins

This pathetic letter to a husband she knew she might never see again, expressing her desperation on seeing her son sold away from her, and her few possessions lost forever—this is, in the end, what captivity meant to the Africans.

It is the dignity of the human reduced to the idea of *thing.* For this is what this woman has become. This is what her child has become. It is a situation that no kind treatment can assuage, a wound of the soul that will never heal.

And what of the wound of the husband and of the child? Could it be less?

Slave trading was a matter of business. Here two dealers, the brothers Silas and R. F. Omohundro, figure their profits. *Alderman Library, University of Virginia*

One way to discover what life was like for the Africans is to look at the plantation records, many of which still exist. We can learn many things from them. From the following records we can see that the owner of this plantation was a careful man, keeping his records from year to year and figuring his profits. We also see that he counted the Africans he held in the same way he counted his other assets.

We see one woman, Betsey, on several lists through the years. We see her first in 1839, then in 1857. In the list for 1860 she is described as "old."

We also see a male named London. In 1839 he is described as a child, then in 1857 he is listed as a house boy.

These are extracts from the plantation records, 1833–1860, of Louis Manigault, owner of the Gowerie and East Hermitage estates near Savannah, Georgia.

(A) General Statement for 1833–1839

I purchased my Savannah River Plantation, Jany, 1833, 220 Acres cleared, 80 uncleared & a fine Rice mill & 50 Negroes for $40,000., viz: the Negroes at $300. each = $15,000. The place $25,000.

I have now April, 1839, Planted & sold six crops.

Sent to market in			
	1833 I made	200	Bbls.
	1834 "	380	[barrels]
	1835 "	294	
	1836 "	389	
	1837 "	404	
	1838 "	578	
		2245	
During these years I made at my mill by Toll		70	
		2315	

Also during these six years I made, but did not sell

Dirty Rice   50
                                                                        2365

My crop this last year averages $4 pr. 100.
But I take $3. as a liberal average for the
last six years.   3. × 6   18
                                                          18920
                                                           2365
                                                          42570

I estimate my Expenses at $2000. per an. for 6
years   12000

Revenue during six years   Dollars   30570

My crop planted last year by 35 hands on 193 Acres
produced of Rice 578 Bbls, average sale $4. × 6= $13,872.00
Also 433½ Bushels Small Rice or 3 Pecks to each
Barrel of Whole Rice at $2. pr. Bush.   867.00
Also 200 Bushels of Peas planted on 16 acres   200.00
And I sold Rice flour from my Mill for   300.00
                                                      15,239.00

But I gave my Negroes the small rice worth $2.50
per bush. instead of Corn which I could have
bought for $1.00 per bush.

Cost of Negroes pr. annum each grown hand
52 Pecks corn, 13 Bushels, at $1. =   13.
Winter and Summer Clothes   7.
Shoes   1.
                                          $21.

77

Negroes at Gowrie, April 1839

Harry (Driver)
Stephen (Miller)
Bina
London (child)
Charles
Juna
Nelly (child)
Nat (Heargrove's child)
Betsey
Paul (born March, 1839)
Matty
George (Cooper)
Peggy
Jack
Tommy
Jacob
Nancy
Bob

Binkey
Amey
Minty
Rihna
Billy (child)
Scotland (child)
Bina (nurse)
Sampson
Kasina
Benty (purchased Feb'y, 1837)
Chalotte (do [ditto])
Sam (child)
Jenny (child)
Scipio
Big Lucy
Ned (trunk minder)
Julia
Sam (cooper)
Moses

Maria
Nanny
Young Ned
Little Lucy
Hanna
Polly (child)
Susey
Martha (child)
Peggy (child)
Fortune
Joaney
Catey
Matty
Chloe
Mary (cook)
Abram
Rachel (cook to overseer)
Hector
Little Charles

Negroes Bought Feby, 1839

Brave Boy, Carpenter, 40 years old
Phillis, his wife, 35
Pompey, Phillis's son, 18
Jack B. Boy & Phillis's son, 16
Chloe child do do
Primus B. Boy's son, 21
Cato Child, B. Boy's son
Jenny (Blind) B. Boy's mother
Nelly's husband in town, 30

Betty, her sister's child who died—child
Affey Nelly's child,—child, 11
Louisa her sister's child who is dead—child, 10
Sarah, Nelly's child, 8
Jack, Nelly's carpenter boy, 18
Ishmel, Nelly's, 16
Lappo Phillis & Brave Boy's, 19

I paid cash for these 16 Negroes, $640. each - $10,240.00

(B) Lists of Negroes, 1857

List of Negroes at Gowrie, this 30th April, 1857

George (Driver)
Betty
Nat
Simon ⎤
and ⎬ (In House)
Polly ⎦
Captain (Chimney
  Sweeper)
Minda
Mathias
Julia
Rhina
Amey and Mary
Harry (With
  Carpenters)
John Izard (Engineer
  and Carpenter)
Judy
Clary
Sary-Ann
Primus

Charles (Trunk
  Minder)
Juna
Jack (Short)
Louisa
Mendoza
Elizabeth & Rebecca
  (Infant 3 weeks)
Scotland
Tommy
Catherine
Phillis
Lucy
Billy (Carpenter,
  little sense)
Jenny
Minty & Scotland
Fortune, runaway
  (Waiting on
  Overseer)
Binah Currie

Hector (Captain,
  Chief boat hand)
Joaney
Tyrah
How-Qua
Fortune, Old
  (Plantation Cook)
Betsey (Carpenter's
  Cook, Nurse)
Cato
Jack Savage (Head
  Carpenter)
London (My House
  Boy)
Nancy Hunt
Abel
George (Carpenter)
Dolly (My Cook and
  Washer)
Lydia (House Girl, 12
  yrs.)

79

List of Negroes at Hermitage, this 30th April, 1857

Ralph (Driver)
Clarinda & Maria
Will (Prime, 28 yrs.)
Klima & Stephney
Nanny (Prime, 28 yrs.)
Abraham 11 yrs.
August 8 yrs.
Parker (Prime, 18 yrs.)
Die, Joe, Rose, Martha
Harriet (Prime, 21 yrs.)
Celim
Bella
Quash
Linda
Clary (Plantation Cook)
William

Cotta
Martha
Pompey
Sarey & Jane
Simon (In house, Cook)
Deborah
Jimmy (Second Engineer, Fireman)
Tilla
Sam (Died of pneumonia, March, 1858)
Bess
Hector
Betty (Brister)
Fortune (Head Bird-Minder with Gun, Prime, 20 yrs.)
Sophy (Prime, 44 yrs.)

Ann (¾ Hand, 22 yrs.)
Charles (Prime, 45 yrs.)
Lucas
Patty (Prime, at times ailing 43 yrs.)
Venus (11 yrs.)
Isaac
Katrina (Prime, 19 yrs.)
July (Prime, 19 yrs.)
Kate (Prime, 18 yrs.)
Andrew (7 yrs.)
Eve (Old, Quite old, cost nothing)
Miley (Prime, 21 yrs.)
Betty (Nurse)

Camp Guardians

Daniel (Old) New Comer, cost nothing. Hannah old.

N.B. Nineteen New Negroes bought this January 13th, 1857, costing $11,850,—being at an average $623.70 for each.

Number Negroes at Gowrie	48
" " East Hermitage	47
" " Camp	2
Total this May 3rd, 1857	97
Prime Hands	54¾

Gave out Summer Clothes this Sunday, May 3rd, 1857

Gave out Winter Clothes this Sunday, December 13th, 1857.

And every Man, Woman & Child has received a blanket, with new born Infants, One Hundred in number.

(C) Lists of Negroes in 1860

List of Negroes at Gowrie, this 22d April, 1860

John

Nancy Hunt

George—Driver

Betty

Minda

Nat

Martha

Julia

Charles (Trunk
  Minder)

Juna

Jack (Short)

Louisa

Mendoza

Tommy

Catherine

Hector (Post Boy)

Joaney (Plantation
  Cook)

Tyrah

Betsey (Old,
  Carpenter's Cook)

Jack, Savage (Chief
  Carpenter)

Amey

John Izard
  (Carpenter, Brick
  Layer)

Clary

Primus

Lucy (With overseer)

Billy (Carpenter)

Jenny

Dolly

Scotland

Fortune (Ran away
  again April, 1860
  Sold in Savannah,
  May, 1860, for
  $1200, as he was
  always running off)

Abel

Binah Currie

Nancy Hunt

George
  (Carpenter,—Run
  away 26th Oct'r.,
  1860; returned

25th, Jany, 1861)

Simon (Run away 2d
  January, 1861;
  returned 25th,
  January, 1861)

Polly & Moses

Lydia

Captain ⎫
  (Drowned ⎪
  in River   ⎬ In
  June, 1860) ⎪ House
Dolly ⎭

Nancy (Gowrie)

Martha (Age 22 yrs.,
  a fine Mulatto
  Woman given me
  by my Father, to
  act as Nurse &c.
  for our child,—Ran
  away in
  Charleston, May,
  1861, caught four
  months after,—no
  longer with me)

81

We purchased in July, 1860 for $500 of Mr. James R. Pringle of Charleston, So. Ca. a Driver named "John" who is at present the only Driver on the Plantation, both George and Ralph, our former Drivers, being broken. Driver John is 44 years of age. Mr. Capers, our Overseer, tells me he has had much trouble with the Negroes the past Summer and several Runaways. Two are now out since October 25th, 1860, and not a word has been heard of them—December, 1860.—Several children died suddenly, the past summer at the Camp.

N.B. I gave blankets to every Man, Woman and Child on the plantation, Dec'r, 1860.

On 25th, January, 1861, all our Runaways (5 in number) were brought in through fear of the dogs. Our Children were poisoned at the Camp by Old Betsey.

From this document we see that there is unrest on the plantation, that there are runaways, and that the drivers George and Ralph have been broken. Then there is the mysterious note that says that the African children were being poisoned by Old Betsey. But another document, a letter to owner Manigault from the white overseer, gives a more complete picture.

June 13, 1860

All things found going on quite well excepting the death of London who was drowned on Monday morning about 9 o'clock. The cause of this sad calamity is this, viz., George brought London & Nat to Ralph, saying they deserved punishment, they were taken to the Barn, when Ralph went for the key to put them in George allowed London to leave him, and when spoken to by Ralph was not making an exertion to stop London his answer was he would not dust his feet to stop him. London went on to Raccoon Square then took the river at the mouth of the canal, in the presence of some of Mr. Barclay's Negroes and Ralph who told him to return [and said that] George should not whip him until my return. His answer was he would drown himself before he would return and he sank soon after, the remains of him in now quite near no 15 Trunk, Gowrie. My orders have been no one is to touch the corpse and [it] will there remain if not taken off by the next tide, this I have done to let the Negroes see when a Negro takes his own life they will be treated in this manner. My advice to you about George is to ship him, he is of no use to you as a driver and is a bad Negro, he would command a good price in Savannah where he can be sold in a quiet manner.

William Capers

London had been raised on the plantation. Had the young man simply had enough? Was death more inviting than yet another beating from the driver? We know that Betsey had known London from the time he was a child on the plantation. How deeply did she mourn his death? Somewhere in the depths of her despair, did she determine that no other African child would be raised to suffer London's fate?

Other records show that George was sold for $1800. There is no record of what happened to Betsey.

9

Fighting Back

The picture often presented of the antebellum South is that of contented Africans living under the kind care of their plantation masters. There were, undoubtedly, some Africans who accepted their lot, having been successfully converted from captive Africans to Negro slaves. A careful look at the records, however, indicates that most Africans longed with all their hearts to be free, and did whatever they could to achieve that freedom. The resistance started as soon as the Africans were captured.

In June 1839, a group of captured Mende Africans were brought from west Africa to Cuba, where they were sold to a pair of Spaniards. On June 28 they were chained belowdecks on a ship, the *Amistad*, to be taken to their destination. On the fourth night at sea the Africans, led by the young man Cinqué,

Cinqué led the revolt on the ship *Amistad. The New Haven Colony Historical Society*

broke their chains and revolted. The captain, the cook, and two sailors were killed. The two men who had purchased the Africans were spared because they convinced the Africans that they would take them back to Africa.

Instead, the two Spaniards changed course often, trying to

reach the United States. On August 26 the ship reached Long Island in New York, where it was boarded by the Coast Guard.

The owners of the ship demanded that the ship be turned over to them, including its human cargo. But under maritime law—the law that concerns the sea and sailing—a ship that was abandoned could be claimed by anyone who found it, and two Americans who first spotted the *Amistad* when it reached Long Island also claimed it.

Meanwhile, local abolitionists took up the cause of the Africans. In a case that was eventually appealed all the way to the Supreme Court, the Africans were declared free. They had not committed a crime against the United States, nor could they be considered pirates as that law was understood. "Suppose they had been impressed American seamen," argued attorney Roger S. Baldwin before the Supreme Court, "who had regained their liberty in a similar manner, would they in that case have been deemed guilty of piracy and murder?"

The answer was no, and the Africans were allowed to go free, returning to Africa in 1842. Cinqué's rebellion had succeeded.

Monday, August 22, 1831. Edmond Drewery, an overseer loading a wagon on the Virginia farm of Jacob Williams, turned as he heard the sound of approaching horsemen. They didn't slow as they neared the house but kept coming quickly. As they got closer, Drewery saw that a young African was leading them. He looked at the others. They were all black.

"Lord! Who is that coming?" he asked of a black woman near him. She didn't know.

Some of the riders were carrying clubs, others axes or swords. The man leading them seemed small in the saddle, with wide shoulders and large, penetrating eyes. The eyes grew larger as he dismounted and lifted his arm. . . .

All the whites on the plantation were killed. The riders finished their grim mission and started toward the next plantation. Before they finished, the Turner band killed fifty-six people. Some were men; many were women and children.

Nat Turner was captured a month after the insurrection and tried in the Southampton community in which he had lived. He was executed on November 11, 1831.

Who was Nat Turner? We'll never know. Reports over the years have tried to discredit his intelligence, and even his sanity. But these reports came from people who did not want to believe that an African who would kill his captors was rational.

Nat Turner changed forever the idea that the Africans were content in their chains. The insurrection in Southampton would be referred to for the next century and a half. If the reality of slavery was cruelty and oppression, its realized nightmare was that the rage of the oppressed would one day erupt into the bloodshed that filled those hot summer days in rural Virginia.

Sometimes Africans could find a way, even in captivity, to earn money. Many had trades from which they earned enough money to save a little. Hundreds of African iron workers, carpenters, shoemakers, and boat pilots put aside precious pennies in hopes of one day buying freedom for themselves and their families. It wasn't easy. An owner might take the money and then change his mind about the agreement. This is what hap-

Some Africans protested silently, others rose up in rage and anger. This drawing of Nat Turner, who led a rebellion in Southampton, Virginia, was made by a local artist after his arrest. *Author*

pened to Josiah Henson, the African who later claimed he was the model for Tom in Harriet Beecher Stowe's antislavery novel *Uncle Tom's Cabin.* His owner agreed upon a price, but when

An African woman, Harriet Henson, agrees to buy her children from Patty Pickerell, who held them. Apparently neither woman could write well enough to sign her name. *Author*

Josiah had accumulated the funds, the owner simply raised the price beyond his reach.

The following document concerns another (unrelated) Henson, a woman who lived in Washington, D.C.

City of Washington
June 22, 1835

Articles of Agreement made and entered into this twenty-second day of June 1835 between Patty Pickerel of Washington City in the District of Columbia of the one part and Harriet Henson of the same place. Witnesseth, That the said Patty Pickerel doth hereby promise and agree to manumit and set free the two children of the said Harriet Henson, Mary and William, as soon as the said Harriet Henson shall pay the sum of six hundred dollars current money, with interest from the date of these presents, to be paid in five annual installments of one hundred and twenty dollars each, And that the said Harriet is to have the use and benefit of the said children during the said time to aid and assist her in raising the money here stipulated to be paid, and the said Harriet Henson doth covenant promise and agree to comply with all stipulations herein contained and to pay the said sum of six hundred dollars and the interest thereon in the manner as above stated. In Witness whereof the parties have hereunto set their hands and seals the day and year aforesaid.

Patty Pickerel
Harriet Henson

Africans could sometimes make arrangements to buy their own freedom or the freedom of family members. In this document Harriet Henson has made an agreement to buy her children from Patty Pickerell (the correct spelling of her name) for

$600. At a time when a dollar a day was considered a fair salary, $600 was a formidable amount.

There were Africans who could neither organize revolts or buy their freedom. Yet freedom was as irresistible to them as to any human being. Many simply ran away, often not knowing where they were going or what awaited them, but being certain that if they were caught, the punishment would be severe. Still, the classified advertisements told of hundreds of men and women who escaped from bondage.

$100 Dollars Reward

Ran away from my plantation, in Bolivar County, Miss., a Negro man named MAY, aged 40 years, 5 feet 10 or 11 inches high, copper colored, and very straight; his front teeth are good and stand a little open; stout through the shoulders, and has some scars on his back that show above the skin plain, caused by the whip; he frequently hiccups when eating, if he had not got water handy; he was pursued into Ozark County, Mo., and there left. I will give the above reward for his confinement in jail, so that I can get him.

—Jefferson (Missouri) Inquirer, Nov. 27, 1852

$25 Reward

Runaway from the subscriber, on or about the first of May last, his Negro boy GEORGE, about 18 years of age, about 5 feet high, well set, and speaks properly. He formerly belonged to Mr. J.D.A. Murphy, living in Blackville; has a mother belonging to a Mr. Lorrick, living in Lexington District. He is supposed to have a pass, and is likely to be lurking about Branchville or Charleston.

Orangeburg (South Carolina), Aug. 7, 1852

FIFTY DOLLARS REWARD—Ran Away from the subscriber, living in Franklin County, North Carolina on the 22nd of January, 1817, a Negro Man named Randol about 26 or 27 years of age, between 5 and 6 feet high, rather yellow complected; appears humble when spoken to. It is expected he has some marks of shot about his hips, thighs, neck and face, as he has been shot at several times. His wife belongs to a Mr. Henry Bridges, formerly of this county. . . .

—*Raleigh (North Carolina) Register*, Feb. 20, 1818

An ad for a runaway African indicates that he had been a metal worker, or smith, in Africa. *Author*

RAN away from the Subscriber of *Frederick* County *(Virginia)* a middle-siz'd Negro Fellow, a little pitted with the Small-Pox, something of the Tawny Complexion, was Imported in 1760, so that he scarcely speaks any *English*, but can work at the Smith's Trade, having been employed in his own Country in that Way. He Eloped the 3d of *April* last with a Wench, that was afterwards taken from him at the *Sugar-Lands* on the *Virginia* Shore, and it's thought he got over into *Maryland*. Any Person that secures him in a Goal, so that I get him, shall have Forty Shillings, or if brought home, Four Pounds, and reasonable Charges, paid by

3   MICHAEL PYKE.

ONE HUNDRED AND FIFTY DOLLARS REWARD.

RUN away the beginning of laſt *September*, from a Mr. *Crocket's* waggon, on its way to *Montgomery* county, 20 miles above the *Rocky Ridge*, a very likely negro woman called HANNAH, about 19 years of age, well ſet, rather ſhort, dreſſes very neat, bred to houſe buſineſs, is of a very paſſionate temper, and when angry, talks very much and faſt. She having a variety of clothes, it is impoſſible to deſcribe her dreſs; and as ſhe is very ſenſible, may endeavour to paſs as a free woman. Aiſo about ſix weeks paſt, a negro lad, about 12 years old, called PHILL, remarkably well made, about 5 feet 6 or 7 inches high, has large lips, a ſly down look, talks little, and generally thick. He formerly belonged to Mr. *John Pryor*, about the time he owned the running horſe Shad, and was well known by being much about with him; had on, when he went away, a dark broadcloth coat, *Virginia* cloth mixed waiſtcoat and breeches, ſtraw hat, yarn ſtockings, ſhoes and ſilver buckles. Having a wife at *Newcaſtle*, I expect he is lurking ſomewhere about that place. I will give 50 dollars for the fellow, and pay reaſonable charges, and 100 for the wench, if taken 50 miles off, and fifty if at a ſmaller diſtance.   WILLIAM DANDRIDGE. Jun.

N. B. I am in want of ſome twine ſpinners and hacklers; ſuch perſons will meet with good encouragement by applying to RICHMOND town, *November* 24, 1779.

Hannah is described as very sensible, while Phill has been sold away from his wife, both good reasons to run off from Mr. Dandridge. *Author*

$20 REWARD—Ran away, about the 15th inst., JOHN CUNNINGHAM. He is about 26 years old, 5 feet 8 inches high, has lost two of his upper teeth in front, also a portion of one little finger, speaks French and English, and calls himself a cook. The above reward will be paid for his delivery in any of the city prisons.

GEO. A. BOTTS New Orleans

Some Americans, who felt that the only way to free the Africans was to send them back to Africa, formed the American Colonization Society. Plantation owners who agreed released their Africans—or arranged in their wills to have them released after the owners had died—but only on condition that they leave the United States and go to Africa. Other Africans, who were already free in the United States, chose to go to Liberia with the Colonization Society. For them, freedom in a society that treated them as second-class citizens was not a true freedom.

On July 4, 1850, the Fuller family started the long journey from Baltimore to Liberia. The Fullers who left on that bright day were John A. Fuller, 26, Paulina Fuller, 19, and 16-year-old Solomon Fuller. A year later John Lewis Fuller would follow with the rest of his children, Roger Fuller and Thomas Fuller, who was 15.

Much of African history is transmitted from generation to generation through oral tradition. Such was the case in the Fuller family. Solomon C. Fuller, Jr., the grandson of the sixteen-year-old Solomon Fuller who migrated to Liberia in 1850, related this story to me in the living room of his Cape Cod home: John Fuller had been a gifted shoemaker and builder who built the first brick house in his section of Norfolk, Virginia. He made fancy shoes as well and earned a great deal of money, most of

Colonization records showing emigration of Fullers from Norfolk, Virginia, to Liberia. Solomon Fuller (#38) is sixteen here. His son returned to the United States, attended one of the freedmen's schools, and married African-American artist Meta Vaux Warrick. *Library of Congress*

<u>Norfolk Va.</u>

15	William H Tyler	27	Laborer	read & writes
16	Martha F. Tyler	23		
17	Richard H. Tyler	7		
18	James O. Tyler	2		
19	Philipa C. Tyler	4		
20	Joseph W. Tyler	1		
21	John A. Fuller	26	Shoemaker	read & writes
22	Paulina Fuller	19		
23	Jasper Boush	32	Farmer	
24	Sarah Boush	21	Washer	
25	Oliver Perry Boushe	1		
26	Henry Nimmo	45	Bricklayer	a little
27	Rebecca Nimmo	30		n. & wr.
28	John H. Nimmo	16	Bricklayer	
29	Maria C. Nimmo	8		
30	Alexander Nimmo	6		
31	Sarah F. Nimmo	4		
32	Tazwell Nimmo	1½		
33	Luke Merchant	26	Blacksmith	a little
34	Penelope Merchant	35	Mantua maker	do
35	John Kempe	31	Painter & glazier	some
36	Sarah Kempe	22		do
37	Maria Cross	18	Washer	
38	Solomon Fuller	16		

<u>Elizabeth City N.C.</u>

| 39 | Sarah Palin | 22 | | |

Lexington &c.

it going to the man who held him. But he was able, by careful management, to save enough to purchase his own freedom and that of his family. A Methodist, Fuller was approached by the Colonization Society in Norfolk and decided that the only place that would be truly free for a man of color would be Africa. He sent his sons first, then followed himself.

Free in Africa, the Fullers soon became successful coffee growers. Thomas Fuller became a Liberian government official; Solomon's son came to the United States to become a noted doctor.

10

George Latimer

The first Africans brought to North America knew nothing about the country, the language, or the customs of the people who held them captive. They were brought here to work in the fields and were easily recaptured when they ran away. But as generations passed, the Africans became familiar with the country and found ways to move around in it. They learned which states were friendly and which were not, and how to travel from one place to another. Although most of the Africans constantly longed for freedom, it sometimes took some special event or act for them to become desperate enough to run away. And running away was a desperate act, for most Africans were caught by either patrollers, bloodhounds, or professional slave catchers. The punishment for running away would almost always be a whipping, and often would be branding or being chained by the neck each night. Some habitual runaways were made to wear heavy iron collars with bells on them. No matter how bad the punishment, there would still be those who ran; someone who had seen her child sold, or who had been separated from his wife.

When Congress stopped the importation of Africans in 1808, the prices being offered for African labor rose dramatically. An industrial advance, the steam-driven textile mill, increased the demand for cotton and, therefore, the need for field workers. A "prime" field hand, meaning a young person in excellent health, was going for over a thousand dollars. The labor of the African had always been valuable, and as the price increased, the Africans themselves were seen as commodities, like gold and real estate are today. A man holding five Africans held five thousand dollars in assets. This led to new kinds of financial dealings involving the captives. Planters would often borrow money from banks using the Africans as collateral, or they would put the Africans up as security for private loans.

The descendants of William Dandridge, who came with his brother John from England to settle in colonial Virginia, furnish an example. Adam Stephen Dandridge II and his brother, Philip Pendleton Dandridge, were great-grandsons of William Dandridge. Their father, Adam Stephen Dandridge I, had inherited a number of Africans from Adam Stephen, his maternal grandfather and the founder of Martinsburg in what is now West Virginia. The descendants of those Africans were then passed on as part of the inheritance of Adam Stephen Dandridge II and his brother, Philip.

The brothers were born at The Bower, a plantation near

Opequon Creek in what was northern Virginia. In 1849, Adam Stephen Dandridge II lived at the Bower and ran the plantation. His brother Philip lived nearby. When Philip needed to secure his loans, he put up part of his inheritance, which consisted of part of the Bower lands, and his Africans.

The following slaves, the property of the said Philip P. Dandridge, now in his possession in Jefferson County, or in the custody of Dr. Gellott Hollingsworth and Samuel Hollingsworth, in the State of Louisiana, together with the increase [children] of said slaves—viz; Cato, Henny, George, Robert, John, Daniel, James, Simon, Peter, Tina, Caroline, Leah, Mary Ann and her children, Rachael, Ann, Louisa & children, Frances, Margaret, Patty, including all of the slaves of the said Philip P. Dandridge, whether named or not . . . to secure a debt of said P. P. Dandridge . . .

It also became obvious that if Africans reproduced, the planters would have greater assets. An owner with large holdings in Africans could make a living simply by selling a number of people each year.

Even so, because this was not the "image" that the plantation owners wanted to present to the world, the yearly sales of Africans were often listed as estate settlements, and some household furniture would be included in the sale. And although most of the sellers denied separating family members, it was clear from the manifests of ships that took Africans from the border states to the deep South that the unattached Africans were being separated from their families.

Great Sale of Slaves.

ON Thursday the 16th of December next, at the Bower Farm in Jefferson county, the late residence of A. S. Dandridge, Esq deceased, the undersigned, executors of Mr. Dandridge, will expose to public sale, at auction, on a credit of twelve months, about

EIGHTY SLAVES,

of both sexes and all ages.

☞ At the same time and place, the Household and Kitchen Furniture, Library, &c. will also be sold at auction, on a credit of 6 months.

Henry St. G. Tucker,
Phil: C. Pendleton,
John R. Cooke.

Nov 11   ts

☞ The editors of the Hagerstown Torch Light, Charlestown Repository, Harpers-Ferry Free Press, and Winchester Republican, will please to insert the above in their respective papers till the day of sale.

The destruction of families "sold South." Ads from the *Martinsburg Gazette* announcing sales by the Dandridge family. *Library of Congress*

Public Sale of Slaves.

FORTY or fifty Slaves will be sold to the highest bidder (with the qualification herein after mentioned) on FRIDAY, the 19th of December next, at the late Mr. Dandridge's

Quarter Farm

in Jefferson county. It is the determination of the undersigned not to sell to any person purchasing with a view to sell again, or with a view to remove the slaves out of the state. A credit of

TWELVE MONTHS

will be given. A number of fine

WORK HORSES

will be sold at the same time and place: Also a quantity of Corn.

Phil. C. Pendleton,   Ex'rs. of
Henry St. G. Tucker,   A. S. Dandridge, dec.
John R. Cooke,

November 20.

☞ The Virginia Monitor, Farmers' Repository, Harpers-Ferry Free Press, the Gazette, and Republican, at Winchester, are requested to insert the above and continue it till sale.

MANIFEST OF SLAVES intended to be transported on board the _Barque_

is Master, of the burthen 277 8/95 tons, and bound from the

this _Tenth_ day of _October_ 1818

	NAMES.	SEX	AGE	STATURE Feet | Inches	COMPLEXION.	SHIPPER'S NAME
1	Julius Woods	Male	25	6	Black	L. Gurley
2	Edmond Jones	do	26	5 8	do	
3	John Williamor	do	22	5 9	do	
4	George Washington	do	18	5 9½	Yellow	
5	Sam Taylor	do	20	5 9	Black	
6	Moses Goodwin	do	25	5 8	do	
7	Noah Coleman	do	18	5 8	do	
8	Peter Lockett	do	22	5 7½	do	
9	Andrew Reid	do	23	5 7½	Brown	
10	George Boling	do	23	5 7	do	
11	Isaih Brouder	do	24	5 7	Black	
12	Roner Still	do	24	5 6¾	do	
13	Henry Jones	do	19	5 5½	do	
14	Hanson Grymes	do	23	5 4½	Yellow	
15	Theodore Grattan	do	19	5 6	do	
16	George Hudnall	do	17	5 6	Brown	
17	Joe Ripley	do	21	5 6½	Black	
18	Allen Fearn	do	17	5 6	Brown	
19	Ephraim White	do	18	5 6	Black	
20	John Smith	do	20	5 5	Brown	
21	Stephen Burton	do	18	5 4½	Black	
22	Dick Lumpkins	do	18	5 6	do	
23	Julius Winston	do	18	5 4½	Yellow	
24	Peyton Threat	do	17	5 4	Black	
25	David Hendrick	do	19	5 3	Yellow	
26	Andrew Jackson	do	17	5 1	Black	
27	Lewis Clifton	do	22	5 8	do	
28	Jacob Wormack	do	23	5 11	Yellow	
29	Caroline Martin	Female	21	5 4½	Brown	
30	Julia H Randolph	do	19	5 9½	Black	
31	Linny McAvoy	do	22	5 3	do	
32	Charlotte Johnston	do	18	5 1½	Brown	
33	Hannah	do	22	5 4	Black	
34	Daphney Ann	do	18	5 1	do	
35	Rosetta Hawkes	do	23	4 11½	do	
36	Harriett Fields	do	17	4 9½	do	
37	Sarah A Fields	do	16	4 10	do	
38	Amy Starke	do	14	4 8	do	
39	Martha Johnson	do	15	4 10½	Yellow	

In Virginia, Maryland, and Kentucky cotton ceased being a major crop. Instead, the economic structure of the South had produced the ultimate in dehumanization: people as product.

A person who held an African, even if he didn't have use for the labor of that person, realized the value he held. An African who escaped was a serious monetary loss.

George W. Latimer was being held in Norfolk, Virginia, by a man named James B. Gray. Latimer's wife, Rebecca, was being held by the DeLacy family and lived not far away. On October 4, 1842, Latimer met his wife—as they had secretly planned—and escaped to Boston, Massachusetts.

But someone who knew him from Virginia saw Latimer in Boston and contacted James Gray in Norfolk.

An ad had appeared in the Norfolk *Beacon* on October 15:

$50 Dollars Reward

Ranaway on Monday night last my Negro Man George, commonly called George Latimer. He is about 5 feet 3 or 4 inches high, about 22 years of age, his complexion a bright yellow, is of a compact well made frame, and is rather silent and slow spoken. . . .

Another ad had appeared for Rebecca Latimer:

Ranaway from the subscriber last evening, negro Woman REBECCA, in company (as is supposed) with her husband, George Latimer, belonging to Mr. James B Gray, of this place. She is about 20 years of age, dark mulatto

Ship's manifest showing the transport of Africans to New Orleans. *Library of Congress*

BY

HEWLETT & BRIGHT.

SALE OF

VALUABLE SLAVES,

(On account of departure)

The Owner of the following named and valuable Slaves, being on the eve of departure for Europe, will cause the same to be offered for sale, at the NEW EXCHANGE, corner of St. Louis and Chartres streets, on *Saturday,* May 16, at Twelve o'Clock, *viz.*

1. SARAH, a mulatress, aged 45 years, a good cook and accustomed to house work in general, is an excellent and faithful nurse for sick persons, and in every respect a first rate character.

2. DENNIS, her son, a mulatto, aged 24 years, a first rate cook and steward for a vessel, having been in that capacity for many years on board one of the Mobile packets; is strictly honest, temperate, and a first rate subject.

3. CHOLE, a mulatress, aged 36 years, she is, without exception, one of the most competent servants in the country, a first rate washer and ironer, does up lace, a good cook, and for a bachelor who wishes a house-keeper she would be invaluable; she is also a good ladies' maid, having travelled to the North in that capacity.

4. FANNY, her daughter, a mulatress, aged 16 years, speaks French and English, is a superior hair-dresser, (pupil of Guilliac,) a good seamstress and ladies' maid, is smart, intelligent, and a first rate character.

5. DANDRIDGE, a mulatoo, aged 26 years, a first rate dining-room servant, a good painter and rough carpenter, and has but few equals for honesty and sobriety.

6. NANCY, his wife, aged about 24 years, a confidential house servant, good seamstress, mantuamaker and tailoress, a good cook, washer and ironer, etc.

7. MARY ANN, her child, a creole, aged 7 years, speaks French and English, is smart, active and intelligent.

8. FANNY or FRANCES, a mulatress, aged 22 years, is a first rate washer and ironer, good cook and house servant, and has an excellent character.

9. EMMA, an orphan, aged 10 or 11 years, speaks French and English, has been in the country 7 years, has been accustomed to waiting on table, sewing etc.; is intelligent and active.

10. FRANK, a mulatto, aged about 32 years speaks French and English, is a first rate hostler and coachman, understands perfectly well the management of horses, and is, in every respect, a first rate character, with the exception that he will occasionally drink, though not an habitual drunkard.

☞ All the above named Slaves are acclimated and excellent subjects; they were purchased by their present vendor many years ago, and will, therefore, be severally warranted against all vices and maladies prescribed by law, save and except FRANK, who is fully guaranteed in every other respect but the one above mentioned.

TERMS:—One-half Cash, and the other half in notes at Six months, drawn and endorsed to the satisfaction of the Vendor, with special mortgage on the Slaves until final payment. The Acts of Sale to be passed before WILLIAM BOSWELL, *Notary Public*, at the expense of the Purchaser.

New-Orleans, May 13, 1835.

PRINTED BY BENJAMIN LEVY.

or copper colored, good countenance, bland voice and self-possessed and easy in her manners when addressed.—She was married in February and at this time obviously [pregnant]. She will in all probability endeavor to reach some one of the free States.

All persons are hereby cautioned against harboring said slave, and masters of vessels from carrying her from this port. . . .

Mary D Sayer

Years earlier Latimer had been held by Edward Mallery, also from the Norfolk area. When Mallery didn't pay his debts—a frequent occurrence—the local sheriff would hold Latimer in jail. The young African boy was worth a great deal of money and would be sold at auction if Mallery did not pay his bills.

. . . I was arrested by the Sheriff, for a debt of my master, Mallery, was put in jail, and stayed there two weeks—had herring and bread for breakfast, and sage tea, and beef alternately, with molasses for dinner every other day. I was flogged once severely, by the jailer, for making noise in my cell. The noise was only the word *Ehue!* an Indian cry, and I only said it three times. Mallery finally bought me out of jail, and returned me back to Mich Johnson, but in a fortnight I was again taken to jail for my master's debts.

[I was sold to] J. B. Gray as a store keeper. I manned his store as a clerk, and did everything but reading and writing. He treated me very badly—as I was knocked and kicked about by him—beaten with a stick and cowhides.

Sales in Southern market: A flyer advertising a sale by the dealers Hewlett & Bright in New Orleans. *The New-York Historical Society*

$50 Dollars Reward.

RANAWAY on Monday night last my Negro Man George, commonly called George Latimer. He is about 5 feet 3 or 4 inches high, about 22 years of age, his complexion a bright yellow, is of a compact well made frame, and is rather silent and slow spoken — I suspect that he went North Tuesday, and will give Fifty Dollars reward and pay all necessary expenses, if taken out of the State. Twenty Five Dollars reward will be given for his apprehension within the State.

His wife is also missing and I suspect that they went off together

or 5 ts   JAMES B GRAY

Ads seeking runaway George Latimer and his young wife. *Norfolk Public Library*

On October 4, however, George Latimer and his young wife, who was indeed pregnant with their first child, stowed away in a ship headed north. Latimer knew ships, and knew that no one would look in the prow of the boat, between the frame of the ship and the sides. There they hid in a small compartment that held the stone weights used as ballast.

The trip from Norfolk took nine hours. All the way the young couple clung to each other. Through the cracks in the bulkhead George could see into the ship's bar, where men were relaxing and drinking. He knew that if any of the Southerners had known that on board there were two Africans trying to escape to the North, they would have hauled him out and put him in irons.

In Boston the Latimers looked for work. George Latimer could do a number of things, including driving a dray—a small wagon—and working as a clerk in a store. Surely, he thought, there would be some work for him in the large city. He didn't know that he had already been discovered.

It was only a matter of days before James B. Gray reached Boston and located the man who had spotted Latimer. Then he went to the sheriff's office and asked that Latimer be arrested on charges of stealing from the grocery store that Gray owned in Norfolk.

The many free Africans in Boston knew what was happening and tried to prevent Latimer's arrest but failed. A group of abolitionists tried to gain Latimer's freedom in court, but because Gray claimed Latimer as a fugitive slave, a judge gave Gray two weeks to prove ownership of Latimer. If he proved ownership, he could then take him back to bondage in Norfolk.

Latimer was locked up by the sheriff while Gray waited for his proof of ownership to arrive from Virginia. The abolitionists, pointing out that Latimer had not been convicted or accused of a crime and should not be held in jail, circulated petitions for his release. They wanted him either released or handed over to Gray without waiting for proof to arrive. In that case, they were willing to take him by force from the Virginian.

Gray knew that he couldn't keep Latimer from the crowds of people who wanted his freedom without the sheriff's help. He offered to sell Latimer, first for a thousand dollars and then for four hundred. The money was raised by the Tremont Temple, a black Baptist Church in Boston, and paid to Gray. For the first

time in his twenty-two years George Latimer was free.

But the toll on Latimer had been a heavy one. He was always afraid of the kidnapers who preyed on the free Africans in the North. Stories circulated about people being dragged from their homes in the middle of the night and put on ships bound for the deep South and a life of captivity. Latimer worked constantly as a house painter, but moved his family with increasing frequency as he felt the possibility of recapture. A stroke left him partially paralyzed, and he died in 1896 a deeply troubled man.

George W. Latimer. *New York Public Library, Schomburg Collection*

11

The Dred Scott Case

In 1812 the United States had a brief war with Great Britain. An important result of the war was decreased trade between the two countries and a marked increase in the industrial capacity of the United States. Almost all the new manufacturing was in the Northern part of the country, which was quickly developing into an industrial power while the South remained basically an agricultural region. To further the development of Northern industries, Congress, controlled by the North, passed tariffs, or taxes on imported manufactured goods. *DeBow's Review*, a major Southern publication of the time, complained that almost everything used in the South was actually manufactured in the North. (*DeBow's Review* itself, published in Louisiana, was printed on Northern presses in New York.)

Cotton was grown in the American South, sold to English

factories, where it was made into clothing, and then sent back to the United States, where it was bought by Americans. By the 1850's, tariffs on the clothing that was brought into the country greatly reduced the profits that the English could make on their products. As a result, the English naturally bought less cotton from the South. Northern factories still bought a great deal of cotton from the South, but since they did not have to compete with English factories, they could buy the cotton cheaper. The industrial North gained by getting cotton cheaper and by reducing the competition from English clothing manufacturers. The tariffs hurt the English factories but not nearly as much as they hurt the producers of the cotton. Southerners complained bitterly about the tariffs but could do nothing about them. The North had the larger population, and therefore the most representatives in Congress. It took Southern support to get new states into the Union, however, and when the Missouri territory applied for statehood in 1820, there was a great debate in Congress. Would Missouri enter the Union as a slave state, and therefore be sympathetic to the South, or as a "free" state with Northern sympathies? The result of the debate was the Missouri Compromise.

The Compromise said that in order to preserve the balance of slave and free states, and thus maintain an equal number of senators on each side, Missouri would enter the Union as a slave state and Maine would enter the Union as a free state. What was more, the rest of the large area of land known as the Louisiana Purchase would be free north of the latitude 36° 30'.

What the South had wanted, along with the admission of

Missouri as a slave state, was enforcement of the fugitive slave provisions of the Constitution. The free states, however, were not at all interested in helping the South regain its runaway Africans. The Latimer case, and ones like it, seemed to the South proof that the differences between North and South were irreconcilable.

Latimer had been helped by Boston abolitionists. Now black abolitionists such as Martin Delaney and Frederick Douglass teamed with whites such as William Lloyd Garrison to agitate against slavery. Lawyers sympathetic to the cause of Africans brought cases to the courts in efforts to free them. The most famous of these cases involved Dred Scott.

John Emerson, a surgeon in the United States Army, held a man named Dred Scott who traveled with him. One of the posts to which he traveled was Fort Snelling, in the territory that had been declared free by the Missouri Compromise. Emerson had then taken him back into Missouri.

Dred Scott was not an educated man. It is doubtful that he could either read or write, but it is certain he was a man who wanted to be free. Presumably he had heard that some Africans who had traveled into free territories had been declared free by the courts. So when people approached him to see if he wanted to sue for his freedom, he said he did.

The circuit court in St. Louis is not far from the busy docks of the Mississippi River. During the summer sessions, it was

Free Africans were often kidnaped, taken to the slave states, and sold. *Library of Congress*

112

CAUTION!!

COLORED PEOPLE

OF BOSTON, ONE & ALL,

You are hereby respectfully CAUTIONED and advised, to avoid conversing with the

Watchmen and Police Officers of Boston,

For since the recent ORDER OF THE MAYOR & ALDERMEN, they are empowered to act as

KIDNAPPERS

AND

Slave Catchers,

And they have already been actually employed in KIDNAPPING, CATCHING, AND KEEPING SLAVES. Therefore, if you value your LIBERTY, and the *Welfare of the Fugitives* among you, *Shun* them in every possible manner, as so many *HOUNDS* on the track of the most unfortunate of your race.

Keep a Sharp Look Out for KIDNAPPERS, and have TOP EYE open.

APRIL 24, 1851.

sometimes almost unbearably hot and humid. The building is attractive, and the intricate ironwork on the staircase is among the best in the state. In those days the courtroom itself was simply furnished, with six chairs placed together on one side of the room for the jury. The tables for the lawyers seemed small in the high-ceilinged room.

Scott's lawyers argued that he had been taken into a free state, a state in which the institution of slavery was illegal. It followed, they argued, that when Dred Scott had resided in that state, he had become a free man. Judges in similar cases had granted Africans their freedom. The time dragged on as the lawyers conducted hearings and the case was tried and appealed. Finally, in 1850, Dred Scott was declared to be a free man.

Dr. Emerson appealed the case to the Missouri Supreme Court, the highest court in the state of Missouri. That court ruled that Dred Scott was still a slave. The judge said that to free Dred Scott would be to set a precedent that would threaten the stability of the country. The judge knew that the Northern lawyers were not just trying to free one man; they were challenging the whole issue of slavery in the territories.

Scott's lawyers then sued in Federal court, claiming that the African's present owner, a man named John Sanford, was a citizen of the state of New York and that Scott was a citizen of Missouri and therefore it was a federal rather than state case. Appeals went to the United States Supreme Court, the highest

Dred Scott. *Library of Congress*

114

court in the land, and was decided on March 6, 1857.

The Supreme Court voted 7–2 against Dred Scott. But the decision, delivered by Chief Justice Roger Brooke Taney, went much further than any previous Supreme Court decision.

Taney firmly believed in slavery. He ruled that Congress did not have the right to prohibit slavery in a territory and therefore declared that the Missouri Compromise was itself illegal.

He didn't stop there. He said that a Negro, slave or free, was not a citizen of the United States and could not become one, and therefore "had no rights which the white man was bound to respect," including the right to sue—meaning that Scott's suit itself was invalid.

Scott's freedom was finally purchased by a group of whites, and he was released. But the significance of the Dred Scott decision extended far beyond Scott himself. Celebrated in the South and reviled in the North, the decision took the fight for the rights of Africans out of the courts. Many Southerners hoped the case would end the rash of lawsuits and legal maneuvering of those opposed to slavery. Instead, Taney's decision served only to harden the positions of North and South.

12

John Brown

What makes an event outstanding? Sometimes it is the effect of what happens; sometimes it is the people who are involved; sometimes it is what people are thinking about when the event occurs. In 1859 the South was at odds with the country and thinking that the presidential candidate of the new Republican party, Abraham Lincoln, was going to make things even worse. Lincoln was clearly against slavery and, as far as Southerners were concerned, against them as well. There was talk of secession if Lincoln was elected.

But as much as Southerners disliked the Republican candidate, they liked the talk of abolitionists less. No one who lived in a place where people held Africans could forget Nat Turner's insurrection in 1831. The possibility that the Africans, stirred up by the abolitionists, would rise up in another bloody insurrection was a constant Southern fear. Abolitionists were simply not welcome in the South, and free Africans were regarded with suspicion. The future of the United States, only seventy-five years old, was in doubt. Any crisis threatened its very existence. The crisis came in the person of a man named John Brown.

John Brown was born on May 9, 1800, in Torrington, Connecticut. His ancestors had come to this country on the *Mayflower*. He had a large family and was barely able to support them as he tried his hand at farming, selling wool, tanning, and land speculating. John Brown was white, but in 1849 he was living in a community largely populated by black people.

Small farmers could not compete with large plantation owners with their African labor. When Kansas was being considered for statehood, it was suggested that the settlers in the territory vote on the slavery issue. The settlers who wanted to avoid the competition from the large planters, along with other antislavery settlers, were called "free soilers."

When John Brown migrated to Kansas in 1855, the area was embroiled in a fierce struggle between those who wanted slavery in the new state and those who were against it. Slaveholders had sent men to Kansas to drive out the antislavery people, and John Brown entered the struggle with a vengeance. He had decided that it was his God-given duty to fight against the people who wanted to hold Africans in bondage.

Responding to a raid on the free soilers, John Brown led a group of armed men against a settlement he considered to be

John Brown. *Library of Congress*

proslavery. Brown's men captured five men and hacked them to pieces. Soon the name of John Brown—or Osawatomie Brown, as he had been nicknamed, after the place in Kansas where the massacre occurred—was feared throughout the border states.

Brown, after his raid in Kansas, decided on an even bolder action. He would first capture the arsenal at Harpers Ferry, Virginia. Then he would take the weapons he had obtained and form a camp in the hills where, he thought, thousands of Africans would escape from the plantations and join him.

In the North the fifty-nine-year-old Brown began to contact black leaders. According to Brown, he contacted abolitionists Frederick Douglass, Henry Highland Garnet, and Harriet Tubman. It is known for sure only that he contacted Douglass, who didn't care much for his ideas. Douglass described a meeting with Brown and some of his men near his home.

Captain Brown, Kagi, Shields Green, and myself sat down among the rocks, and talked over the enterprise about to be undertaken. The taking of Harper's Ferry, of which Brown had merely hinted before, was now declared his settled purpose, and he wanted to know what I thought of it. I at once opposed it with all the arguments at my command. To me, such a measure would be fatal to running off slaves (the original plan), and fatal to all engaged. When about to leave, I asked Green what he had decided to do, and was surprised by his saying, in his broken way, "I believe I'll go with the old man."

Brown also contacted a number of white abolitionists, whose

Frederick Douglass. *Library of Congress*

reactions to his plan were mixed. But he did collect sufficient funds to start his operation. It has never been clear that any of the white abolitionists knew the details of Brown's plans for October 16, 1859.

There wasn't a lot to do in Harpers Ferry on a Sunday evening. The big attraction was having a meal or a drink at the Wager Hotel. Some soldiers from the arsenal were at the hotel's bar, trying to relieve the boredom of weekend duty. There were a few whites around and a few Africans from nearby plantations. The old black man leaning against the bridge that led to the arsenal was dozing off.

Brown's band consisted of twenty-one men; sixteen were white and five black. Among the whites were his own two sons, carrying weapons they hid under their coats. They broke up into small groups and drifted into town slowly, trying to appear casual.

Guards were posted on the bridge leading toward the arsenal, but most of the soldiers on duty, not expecting any trouble, were either in town at the hotel bar or had drifted off. A black man named Heyward, sensing that something was wrong, tried to give the alarm and was shot down. The attack was on. Brown's men moved in quickly and captured several buildings.

The firing could be heard coming from the arsenal, and the town was soon in an uproar. What was happening? Some thought it was just soldiers shooting off their guns at a luckless possum. Slowly the people of Harpers Ferry began to put the pieces together. Somebody had attacked the arsenal. Hostages had been taken, including Colonel Lewis Washington, great-grandnephew of George Washington.

Many of the shots were wild as townspeople and raiders exchanged fire. Brown gave orders to his "soldiers," but there was a great deal of confusion. A raider fell dead in the street. Some of the raiders were in the arsenal, while others herded the hostages they had rounded up into a small building known as the engine house, which contained fire-fighting equipment. It had two rooms; the one the raiders were in measured about seventeen feet wide and sixteen feet deep. When the two heavy wooden doors were closed, it was dark inside. The raiders shot through the high side window when they could see someone. Other than that they had to open the front door to shoot out. Bullets slammed against the door on a regular basis, but none penetrated.

When the mayor of Harpers Ferry, a much-respected man by the name of Fontaine Beckham, tried to approach the engine house in which Brown and his men were concealed, he was shot dead instantly.

George Turner, a wealthy farmer and the owner of the nearby Wheatland plantation, went to see what the excitement was all about. He was hit by a bullet that ricocheted through his body, and he fell mortally wounded.

A marksman shot through the open engine house door and killed another raider.

Sporadic firing lasted through the night. There were rumors about who the raiders were, and how many of them were firing. By the next morning there was only one thing that was absolutely clear: A federal arsenal had been attacked. A telegram

Harpers Ferry. The engine house is the building in the left foreground. *Harpers Ferry Archives*

was sent to the White House.

James Ewell Brown Stuart, known as J.E.B. or Jeb Stuart, a young lieutenant who happened to be in Washington trying to get a patent on an invention he had just completed, was dispatched to take a message to Colonel Robert E. Lee of the United States Army.

The day stretched on, and the excitement in Harpers Ferry rose as it became clear that the raiders were still in the arsenal. A message was delivered from the engine house. Calling himself "Mr. Smith," the leader of the raiders demanded food and drink.

The food was delivered from the nearby Wager Hotel, but the raiders, now believing that the food was drugged, were afraid to eat it.

Lee was at his home near Arlington, Virginia when J.E.B. Stuart arrived with the news of the attack. A special locomotive was sent to take the two men to Harpers Ferry. A detachment of Marines was also sent.

It was Monday, October 17. Lee and Stuart had arrived in Harpers Ferry and were surveying the scene. The mob around the arsenal fired shots almost randomly at anything inside that moved. The bodies of several raiders who had already been killed were being used by the townspeople for target practice.

Conditions inside the engine house were nearly unbearable. One of John Brown's sons lay dead, the other was dying. The hostages cowered in the corners. The uneaten food lay scattered about the floor. The men had no place to relieve themselves except the floor, and the smell of urine and sweat filled the darkness.

One of the white raiders, a tall man named Thompson, had been wounded in the street and taken into the Wager Hotel. He had been briefly questioned, and the next proposal was to kill him.

Christine Fouke, sister of the Wager's manager, put her body between Thompson and his would-be executioners.

"Don't kill him in that way," she cried. "Let the law take its course!"

But the assembled crowd dragged the bound man out of the room and shot him over forty times.

Colonel Lee directed Lieutenant Stuart to deliver a message to Mr. Smith. He and his men were to release the hostages and surrender at once.

When Stuart approached the engine house with Lee's demands and the door opened, Stuart recognized "Mr. Smith" as Osawatomie Brown from the Kansas raids.

Brown demanded that he and his men be allowed to leave the engine house and the town and that they not be followed. In return he would see that the hostages would not be harmed.

Stuart refused to entertain the idea. Brown said that he would as soon die from a bullet as on the gallows. On a signal from Stuart the Marines began battering down the door to the arsenal. When it broke, they rushed in. One crumpled at the door as a bullet hit his stomach.

In order not to injure the hostages, the Marines attacked with rifle butts and bayonets. Brown was clubbed down to the ground, and the remaining raiders were quickly captured and taken to a nearby building.

Brown was badly wounded but still alive as a New York *Herald* reporter hurriedly took notes.

"Captain Brown, what brought you here?" John Brown was asked as he lay wounded.

"To free your slaves" was the prompt reply.

"How did you expect to do it, with the small force you brought?"

"I expected help."

"From whites as well as blacks?"

"I did."

126

"Then you have been disappointed in not getting it."

"Yes."

"Will there be more attempts to cause the slaves to rise up?"

"Time will tell" was the answer.

John Brown was questioned closely about his support. He had been given money by a number of Northern abolitionists. One of those who supported him with money (but later claimed not to have known about the raid) was Dr. S. G. Howe, whose wife, Julia, would later write the words to "The Battle Hymn of the Republic."

John Brown fulfilled the worst nightmare of the South. Here was a white man who was prepared to bring guns to the Africans. His raid led many Southerners to believe that it was just a matter of time before other Northerners would try to use force to free all the Africans.

What was the meaning of the raid on Harpers Ferry? The first reports from *The New York Times* reported it as simply a nonpolitical raid on the arsenal. Most Northern newspapers condemned the raid and the killings as the work of madmen. But there were people who saw other significance in John Brown's activities; one of them was Governor Henry Wise of Virginia. Brown could have been tried for murder and quickly dispatched, but Wise chose to have him tried for insurrection, thereby turning the raid itself into a political action. Soon newspapers from all over the country were sending reporters to Charles Town, where Brown was being held. He was allowed to give lengthy statements to the press; he was given writing materials, and his letters, too, would be made public. Abolitionists recognized that Brown was going to become a martyr and rallied, at least in print, to his cause.

Brown's trial was held in the courthouse in Charles Town. It was crowded with onlookers and press reporters from throughout the country. Men jostled for a clear view of the proceedings, claiming special rights to be at the trial they sensed was making history. Brown, still recovering from the wounds he had received when the Marines stormed the engine house, lay on a cot near the front of the court. There were times when his suffering was apparent; other times he lay quietly listening to the proceedings. At no time did he deny what he had done. Trying to save him, his lawyers claimed that insanity ran in his family, but Brown denied that he was insane. He was found guilty and sentenced to death.

On December 2, 1859, Brown spent his last hours writing letters. He had already said good-bye to his wife. Rumors of a Northern plot to free Brown had circulated through the town, and outside the jail there were soldiers everywhere.

A wagon ten feet long was brought to the steps of the jailhouse. Inside the wagon there was a coffin. There were troops behind it and in front of it, and a mounted army officer nervously looked over the street, keeping civilians back from the scene. Finally Brown and the sheriff came through the doors of the jail and went directly to the wagon. Brown's arms were tied to his sides and his hands cuffed behind him. No one was allowed within thirty feet of him. He sat on the coffin and in seconds was on his way to the gallows.

Just outside of town soldiers surrounded the newly built gallows, and an artillery team checked the aim of the cannon that was trained on the spot where Brown would stand.

"This is beautiful country," Brown said as the plain cart moved through the streets of Charles Town.

Brown went to his death without flinching and without crying out. After the execution there seemed to be an air of disappointment in Charles Town. None of the plots to free "the old man" had materialized. The raid had failed, and its leader was dead. Newspaper reporters searched out the officials who had attended the execution, looking for bits of news to put into their stories. Someone made up a story that Brown had stopped on the way to the gallows to kiss a black child, and by late afternoon it was being sent around the country as truth.

On the Wheatland plantation the white family was still mourning the death of George Turner at Harpers Ferry. Four-year-old Louisa Jackson wouldn't have known what the excitement was about. The brown-skinned, wide-faced girl listened to the grown-ups whispering behind the smokehouse and talking about somebody by the name of John Brown. She didn't know who John Brown was, only that he had somehow caused the death of George Turner, the man who had owned the plantation and the other black people who lived there with her.

After the execution of Brown a number of mysterious fires broke out on the Wheatland and neighboring plantations. But in beautiful Harpers Ferry, where the Potomac River meets the Shenandoah, the conflict, for the moment, had ended.

13

Secession

John Brown was dead, but the cause he had fought for lived on. Northern papers, which had at first condemned the raid at Harpers Ferry, ran statements from abolitionists, and Northern poets wrote eulogies to Brown. The result was anti-Southern feeling in the North, and a total lack of support for programs designed to help the ailing Southern economy. Southern papers retaliated by ridiculing the "Yankees."

The only way to be elected president in 1860 was with the support of the North, and both candidates, Abraham Lincoln and Stephen A. Douglas, courted Northern votes. Neither was fully acceptable to the South, but Douglas might have been tolerated. But on November 7, 1860, the headlines across the nation announced the news that Abraham Lincoln had become the sixteenth president of the United States.

Three days later South Carolina called a secession convention. The senators from South Carolina resigned from the Senate.

Major Robert Anderson was commander of Fort Sumter, a federal fort in South Carolina. Clearly seeing an armed conflict ahead, he made an urgent call for supplies and reinforcements, but outgoing President Buchanan did not reply. On December 20, South Carolina became the first state to secede from the Union. On January 9 Mississippi seceded. They were followed on the tenth by Florida. By the end of the month Alabama, Georgia, and Louisiana had also seceded.

In a last-ditch effort to prevent the breakup of the Union, Senator Crittenden of Kentucky proposed six amendments to the Constitution that would protect slavery. These amendments were rejected by the Senate.

Virginia, largely pro-Union, offered peace proposals that were also rejected by the Northern-controlled Congress.

On April 12, 1861, the newly formed Confederate States of America fired upon Fort Sumter. The War of the Rebellion had begun.

––––––––––

The War Between the States has also been called the War of the Rebellion, the Civil War, and the War of Southern Independence. The newly formed Confederacy thought of itself as a separate nation with interests distinct from those of the United States. For the Confederacy the war was an effort to gain its independence. But for Lincoln and the North the war was an act of rebellion, pure and simple.

The reasons for the war were probably most clearly to be found in the questions left unanswered during the very formation of the United States.

We the people of the United States, in order to form a more perfect union, establish justice, insure domestic tranquility, provide for the common defense, promote the general welfare, and secure the blessings of liberty to ourselves and our posterity, do ordain and establish this Constitution of the United States of America.

What was the purpose of "a more perfect union"? Was it truly to "promote the general welfare, and secure the blessings of liberty to ourselves and our posterity"? And who *were* "We the people"? Chief Justice Roger Taney had determined, in the Dred Scott decision, that "the people" did not include those of African descent.

And "the general welfare" of the South depended largely on the "peculiar institution" of slavery and relief from tariffs.

And what would happen if the sectional interests of so large a country as the United States developed differently? If the North had different needs from the South, or the East had different needs from the West? The Constitution did not answer this question.

(Most Africans, captive and free, welcomed the war. They believed that whatever the other reasons for the war, a Northern victory would mean their freedom.)

An important career opportunity for young men in the South was the military. Some of the best minds of the South were to be found in the military academies, and by the beginning of the war a major advantage for the South was the quality of its officers.

The South also had an advantage in its people. The men of the South were used to its terrain. Accomplished horsemen and skilled marksmen, the Rebels, as they were called, handily defeated the Union forces in the first battles of the war.

Another important element in the Confederacy was the morale factor. Although it was the South that fired the first meaningful shots in the war, it was the North that invaded Southern strongholds. The South was defending its own territory, its own principles. Yet another element, one that few had expected to be an important part of the war, was the support of their army by Southern women.

Northern women, in their writings and pleas to end slavery, had helped to create much of the anti-South atmosphere. But once the war began, it was Southern women who held up the morale of the South and urged its men on.

In the beginning few people in the South thought that they could win a war with the Union. From a military viewpoint they could only hope that the North would have no stomach for a full-scale war. There was also the hope that the Confederacy would be recognized as an independent country by the rest of the world, especially England, which needed Southern cotton. Perhaps England could even be persuaded to assist the South.

While the South had the advantage of excellent leadership, soldiers defending their own homelands, and men used to both the terrain and handling weapons, the North also had its advantages.

The major advantages of the North were its industrial might and its much larger population. A fully mobilized federal force could be twice the size of the largest Confederate army. The shape of the war soon became obvious. It was Southern daring, strategy, and fighting ability against superior Northern numbers and supplies.

Some Southern military strategists thought that if the South did not win quickly, the next-best thing would be to prolong the war until the North, fighting under the disadvantage of sending its men miles from their homes, would tire of the fighting and ask for peace.

The first battles raised the spirits of the South. The Rebels defeated a poorly led, overconfident Union army, inflicting casualties in the thousands. Southern papers proclaimed victory after victory.

These were Americans fighting Americans. In many cases it was neighbors fighting neighbors, brothers against brothers.

The South formed the Confederate States of America, which included South Carolina, Mississippi, Florida, Alabama, Georgia, Louisiana, Texas, Virginia, Arkansas, North Carolina, and Tennessee. The Confederacy argued that the original formation of the United States was only an agreement among states, an agreement that could be later changed. Jefferson Davis was chosen to be the Confederacy's first president.

A small section of Virginia refused to secede, and was quickly recognized by the Union as the state of West Virginia. It would be officially admitted as a state in June 1863.

The constitution of the Confederate States addressed clearly the question of slavery. "No . . . law denying or impairing the right of property in Negro slaves shall be passed."

Lincoln, in his first inaugural address, responded to the secessionists:

> The power confided to me will be used to hold, occupy, and possess the property and places belonging to the government and to collect the duties and imposts.

Lincoln said, in effect, that the Union forces would go to war against the Confederacy to hold the Union together.

The attitudes of the North at the beginning of the war varied greatly. New York City, fearing that it would suffer severe financial losses, threatened to secede and remain neutral. In July 1863, some white New Yorkers in poor neighborhoods responded bitterly to the draft, thinking they should not have to risk their lives to fight for the freedom of Southern blacks. During the riots that followed, many Africans were killed and the New York Colored Orphans Home on Fifth Avenue was burned down. Other Northerners thought the war would be over quickly, that the Rebels would be taught a lesson and things would return to normal. This made the possibility of war seem tolerable.

Congress passed a resolution stating that the war was about preserving the Union, not freeing the Africans, and it was passed without opposition.

——— ———

Southerners in the United States Army had a tough choice to

make. They had sworn to defend the United States, and now they were being asked to invade their own states, to fight against people who were their relatives, their friends, their neighbors. Colonel Robert E. Lee, who had defended the Harpers Ferry arsenal against John Brown's raiders, was offered a promotion. After much agonizing he felt that he could not turn against his native Virginia, and resigned his commission in the United States Army.

Young men in the South were convinced that they could repel

Work pass. The Confederates used Africans to build fortifications. *Author*

Richmond, Va. Apr. 12 186 2

Received of E. McDaniel

the following slaves, viz: Tyler

for work on fortifications at and near this City.

By order Lt. Col. W. H. STEVENS,

Chief Engineer D. N. V.

Government Agent.

Powder monkey during the Civil War carried gunpowder for the cannons up from a ship's hold. *National Archives*

the Yankee invaders and volunteered in great numbers for the Confederate Army.

Frederick Douglass, who had been born in captivity and had escaped to the North, urged Lincoln to allow the Africans to fight. He was ignored.

The Southern war effort was both remarkable and heroic. The War of Southern Independence took on the trappings of a holy war.

But even as they won battles, Southern generals realized they were losing more than they could afford. With less manpower, less money, and less industrial strength than the North, they could not win without help.

The South still supplied the cotton for the mills of England. Without a steady supply of cotton the English economy would eventually suffer. But both the French and the English were wary of entering the American war. Both waited to see if the South really had a chance to win before making a commitment.

From the outset Africans in the South had been forced into the Southern effort. They built the fortifications, cooked, tended the animals, carried supplies, and did the hundreds of jobs that freed white Southern soldiers to fight.

The soldiers, on both sides, were from all walks of life. There were clerks, shopkeepers, farmers, blacksmiths, tailors, and schoolboys In Philadelphia recruiters went to schools and took high school boys by the class. They were considered graduates if they went off to fight.

14

The Bower

J.E.B. Stuart was born on February 6, 1833. His father had fought in the War of 1812 and his great-grandfather in the Revolutionary War. The young lieutenant had been in Kansas when John Brown and his sons made their famous raids against the proslavery forces.

Stuart had been stationed in the west, where he had combat experience fighting against Native Americans. Lee needed all the experienced men he could get and quickly accepted the young cavalry officer into his command. Stuart knew northern Virginia and knew he could use his horsemen to supply Lee with information about the enemy. His chance came quickly as Lee asked him to check on the size and strength of McClellan's Union forces. Instead of merely probing McClellan's flanks, as most officers would have done, Stuart, in a hard ride, rode com-

pletely around the Union Army, destroying supplies, capturing Union soldiers, and supplying Lee with extraordinary details about his Northern foe.

It was this kind of daring and dedication that carried General J.E.B. Stuart to fame. The successes of Stuart and the Confederacy during this Virginia campaign led many Southerners to believe they could win the war.

In the North enlistments were flagging. Morale was low. Lincoln needed something to turn the tide of the war. He presented a plan to his cabinet: a proclamation of emancipation freeing the Africans in the Confederacy. There was instant opposition to the proposed proclamation, which would make it appear that the war was about freeing the Africans rather than saving the Union. Lincoln decided to postpone the announcement of the plan until the North had won at least one major victory.

On September 17, 1862, McClellan's Union forces finally won a battle against Lee's Army of Northern Virginia. At Antietam, in a fierce struggle that pitted 46,000 Union against 40,000 Confederate troops, Lee received a tactical defeat. He lost 10,000 men to the 12,000 lost by the Union. At the height of the battle almost all of Lee's men were engaged, while the Union had nearly 30,000 soldiers in reserve. Lee prudently withdrew.

On September 22 Lincoln announced the Emancipation Proclamation. It would take effect on the first day of January 1863.

The Emancipation Proclamation did not free all Africans. It

J.E.B. Stuart, one of the Confederacy's ablest generals and its most romantic, spent some time relaxing at The Bower, the Virginia home of Adam Stephen Dandridge II. *Eleanor S. Brockenbrough Library, The Museum of the Confederacy* freed only those Africans who were being held by the states that were in rebellion against the United States. Exceptions to the Proclamation included Africans who lived in parts of Louisiana, parts of eastern Virginia, and all of West Virginia.

The effect of the Emancipation Proclamation was enormous. A direct attack on the social structure of the South, it was meant to demoralize the South, and to a large extent it did. Africans who could escape from their masters and find their way to Union lines would be free. This encouraged the Africans to rise up against their owners. If the Union won the war, there would be a virtual end to slavery in the United States.

The word spread quickly from plantation to plantation. Scores of black people left the fields, the Rebel camps, and Southern cities in search of the Yankees and freedom. Southerners who had long feared an African uprising now realized that the possibilities of one grew every day. Editorials in Southern papers denounced Lincoln as never before.

Southern politicians also noted the positive reaction to the proclamation in England, which had outlawed slavery in its colonies in 1833. All hope for English aid to the Confederacy was lost.

The North had resisted using Africans as soldiers. Some whites said that the Africans were too accustomed to being

The Emancipation Proclamation was carefully worded to avoid antagonizing the border states of Kentucky, Maryland, Missouri, and West Virginia. *Library of Congress*

By the President of the United States of America:

A Proclamation.

Whereas, on the twenty-second day of September, in the year of our Lord one thousand eight hundred and sixty-two, a proclamation was issued by the President of the United States, containing, among other things, the following, to wit:

"That on the first day of January, in the "year of our Lord one thousand eight hundred "and sixty-three, all persons held as slaves within "any State or designated part of a State, the people "whereof shall then be in rebellion against the "United States, shall be then, thenceforward, and "forever free; and the Executive Government of the "United States, including the military and naval "authority thereof, will recognize and maintain "the freedom of such persons, and will do no act "or acts to repress such persons, or any of them, "in any efforts they may make for their actual "freedom.

"That the Executive will, on the first day

dominated by white men to fight them; others thought Africans weren't agile enough to fight. But the North needed fresh troops, and so a plan was devised to accept Africans into the Union Army.

In September 1862, J.E.B. Stuart was in fine spirits. He was in western Virginia at the plantation home of Adam Stephen Dandridge II. The Dandridges were cousins to John Esten Cooke, who served on Stuart's staff.

The people in this group from Louisiana all share a degree of African ancestry. *New York Public Library, Schomburg Collection*

The Bower today. *Author*

Edmund Dandridge, one of the Dandridges' sons, was in the 2nd Regiment of the Virginia Infantry and had been wounded at the Battle of Bull Run. Two other Dandridge boys, Adam Stephen III and Lemuel, had also enlisted in the cause of the Confederacy.

The Bower was located a short ride from Harpers Ferry and a short ride from Martinsburg, West Virginia. The big house was modest by Southern-mansion standards, but the Dandridges were well known for their hospitality.

Heros Von Borcke, another of Stuart's staff officers, recorded the stay in a series of articles he wrote about his war experiences:

145

Every evening the Negroes would ask for the lively measures of a jig or a breakdown, and then danced within the circle . . . like dervishes or lunatics, the spectators applauding to the echo.

When General Stuart had finished his paperwork for the day, he would join in the festivities that seemed to be going on constantly. The Bower was filled with young girls, Southern belles attracted to the dashing cavalry officers.

Each night there was dancing. Stuart arranged for musicians, especially the celebrated banjo player Bob Sweeney, to play his favorite songs. According to his biographer, W. W. Blackford, Stuart "loved to kiss a pretty girl, and the pretty girls loved to kiss him." Many people came from nearby towns to join in the celebration.

Mary Boykin Chesnut was the wife of Colonel James Chesnut, an aide to Jefferson Davis, president of the Confederacy. Her diary is one of the most human documents to come out of the war. In it she discusses the progress of the conflict, the bravery of the Confederate soldiers, and the remarkable sacrifices that were being made in the South as Union forces invaded. In expressing her feelings about slavery's effect on white women, she also reveals much about the way African women were used. (The Legree she speaks of is Simon Legree, the evil slave driver in *Uncle Tom's Cabin* by Harriet Beecher Stowe.)

The Dandridges were pleased that some of the Africans joined in the merriment to entertain J.E.B. Stuart; they were less pleased when some of them went off with the Union Army. *London Illustrated News*

I hate slavery. You say there are no more fallen women on a plantation than in London, in proportion to numbers; but what do you say to this? A magnate who runs a hideous black harem with its consequences under the same roof with his lovely white wife . . . ? You see, Mrs. Stowe did not hit the sorest spot. She makes Legree a bachelor.

Throughout her diary Mrs. Chesnut, whose sympathies lay solely with the Confederacy, was as brutally honest about Southern life and about the war as she could be. She felt the pain of the wounded Confederate officers, such as General John Bell Hood and Heros Von Borcke, who rode with J.E.B. Stuart. But she did not like the idea of slavery, especially the vulnerability of African women on the plantations, what she called the "black harem."

When Stuart decided that his men needed a rest, he stayed at The Bower, the home of Adam Stephen Dandridge II, known as Stephen. His stay at The Bower is one of the most romantic pictures of the Civil War offered to us. Many authors, including Heros Von Borcke—who met Mrs. Chesnut—wrote of Stuart's days of relaxation at the secluded mansion near the Opequon Creek. Bob Sweeney played his banjo while Stuart sang and entertained the ladies. The Confederate officers staged plays that delighted the crowds that gathered for the gala balls. Artists from America and Europe made sketches for their newspapers of the dancing Africans and the gracious living even though the war was only a few miles away. This was worth fighting for, a pleasant view of the "old South" that many Southerners used for justifying their way of life. Genteel masters taking care of

148

contented blacks, usually singing or dancing, was the image often presented.

Ironically, the first novel to present this idyllic picture of the South was written by John Pendleton Kennedy, a novelist who had spent much of his youth at The Bower as the guest of his uncle, Adam Stephen Dandridge.

Kennedy would go on to write *Swallowbarn*, published in 1832 and considered the first romantic novel about the South. In it he described the area in which the Africans lived:

Nothing more attracted my observation than the swarms of little Negroes that basked on the sunny sides of these cabins, and congregated to gaze at us as we surveyed their haunts. They were nearly all in that costume of the golden age which I have heretofore described; and showed their slim shanks and long heels in all the varieties of their grotesque natures, from the most knock-kneed to the most bandy legged. Their predominant love of sunshine, and their lazy, listless postures, and apparent content to be silently looking abroad, might well afford a comparison to a set of tarapins [turtles] luxuriating in the genial warmth of summer, on the logs of a mill pond.

And there, too, were the prolific mothers of this redundant brood,—a number of stout Negro women who thronged the doors of the huts, full of idle curiosity to see us. And, when to these are added a few reverend, wrinkled, decrepit old men, with faces shortened as of with drawing strings, noses that seemed to have run all to nostril, and with feet of the configuration of a mattock, my reader will have a tolerably correct idea of this Negro-quarter, its population, buildings, external appearance, situation and extent.

Somewhere on the Dandridge estate, as Stuart's men were enjoying the hospitality of Stephen Dandridge, there was also a

149

little girl named Dolly whose job it was to take care of the many babies produced in the quarter. She was of African descent but very fair skinned, listed on later census records as a mulatto.

In trying to imagine what life must have been like for Dolly, I have to consider her age. At twelve she would not yet be one of the breeding women whom Kennedy described, but she would be approaching an age at which she could be sold at a good price. Her parents were still at The Bower. Perhaps they were, for some reason, in special favor, and therefore had not been sold.

Dolly was described as "just about" white and more than a little strange. But the people telling the story knew her only as an old woman who had lived through more than most people; she could be forgiven for being a little eccentric.

In 1938 her brother Lucas, in an interview with a government employee, claimed that as an eighteen-year-old he had seen John Brown shortly after the famous raid on Harpers Ferry. Whether Lucas Dennis actually did or not is impossible to know.

It is true that Lucas settled in Harpers Ferry once he was free and spent most of his life there. He married Louisa Jackson, the young child who had been held on the Wheatland Plantation whose owner had been killed by John Brown's men during the raid. Louisa was my great-great-aunt.

Much of African-American history has never been written down but has been passed from generation to generation in quiet family gatherings. I first learned of the horrors of African

While my great-grandmother Dolly Dennis was held at The Bower, another great-grandmother, Mary Hardin, was also being held in Jefferson County, West Virginia. She's shown here with my grandmother Gertrude Williams. *Author* captivity while helping my mother snap beans in a Harlem tenement. The stories were not just information; they scared me so badly I couldn't sleep at night for thinking about them. It pained me to know that so many in my family had shared this experience. Dolly was from my mother's family, but I remember my grandfather on my father's side telling us how he knew his age.

"I was born just before the war," he said. "They didn't allow none of us to do no reading or writing, but my mama took a newspaper, folded it up, and saved it so she could remember how old I was. After the war she folded the front page of that paper up and put it in the Bible."

I tried to imagine him, small, bright-eyed and sprightly, as a slave, but I couldn't.

But I have been to The Bower, and I have walked among the same oak trees that my great-grandmother, Dolly Dennis, must have seen when she was there. I wonder what she thought when she saw General Stuart and the other Confederate officers. I choose to think that she understood the importance of the war, and of the events at the Dandridge home. I want to believe that she and the other Africans felt the pain inherent in the contrasts between the Africans in the Quarter and the courtly Dandridge family even as they became part of the entertainment. I know from family stories that she loved the babies that she cared for.

Dolly is part of the heritage of all African Americans and of my family in particular. It is a heritage I deeply cherish.

15

We Look Like Men of War

By mid-1862 it was obvious that the war would not be a quick victory for either side. Men were dying by the tens of thousands, and the only clear method of waging the war from the viewpoint of the Union was through the loss of tens of thousands more. Some Northerners were already calling for an end to the war.

In the South morale was still incredibly high. Southerners, in defense of their homes and families, were fighting with ferocity and daring, often carrying the fight to cautious Union generals.

On the other hand, Union soldiers, hardened by months of warfare, were catching up with their Confederate foes in horsemanship and learning more about supplying their troops in the field.

A decision was made to attack Southern morale. Generals like William Tecumseh Sherman and David Hunter began practicing what they called "total war"—attacking civilian as well as military targets, trying to make life in the South so difficult that the Confederacy would lose the support of its people. Union soldiers in the deep South set fire to crops, looted and burned homes, and destroyed livestock. In the Shenandoah Valley General David Hunter burned down the house of his cousin Andrew Hunter, who had been the prosecutor at the John Brown trial.

By the end of 1862 President Lincoln knew he needed more manpower to bring the war to a close. He called for more soldiers and authorized the use of Africans in the Union Army. It was decided to refer to the Africans as "colored," and the regiments in which they served were called United States Colored Troops.

Besides increasing the size of the Union forces, the use of African troops also served to further disrupt Southern life. Every African in the fields was now a potential soldier. Men who carried hoes from sunup to sundown might soon be carrying rifles. What's more, Southerners sensed that fighting for freedom was an idea that, once planted in the mind of an unfree man, would never die. The idea of slavery was forever dead when the first guns were placed in the hands of men determined to be free.

Jefferson Davis, president of the Confederacy, objected strongly to the Union's use of Africans as soldiers and declared that African soldiers captured by the Confederacy would not be treated as prisoners of war. White Union soldiers captured would be humanely treated and either exchanged or put into camps until the war ended, but Africans would be treated as slaves and either returned to their masters or sold. The Richmond newspapers suggested an even stronger course of action: No soldiers of African descent should be taken prisoner; they should be killed.

Further, the Confederate congress passed an act against white officers who led African troops into battle:

That every white person being a commissioned officer, or acting as such, who, during the present war, shall command Negroes or mulattos in arms against the Confederate States . . . shall, if captured, be put to death or be otherwise punished at the discretion of the Court.

Normally, armies try to set up rules of warfare. These rules often deal with the treatment of civilians, of the sick and wounded, and of prisoners of war. From the viewpoint of the Confederacy, however, Africans could not be treated as prisoners of war. Suppose, for example, there were five Africans being held on a plantation and one escaped and joined the Union Army. If he were recaptured and put into a prison camp instead of being immediately shot, would this not encourage the other four Africans on the plantation to run away and join the Union Army too? That this was true was clear to both sides.

Would Africans volunteer to fight if to do so meant certain death if captured? Were they capable of being effective soldiers? Many whites, in both the North and South, felt the Africans did not have the nerve to stand up to the rigors of combat. Many Union soldiers and officers declared they would not want to rely on African soldiers. Nevertheless, the Army decided to put together all-black regiments with white officers. One of the first of these was the 54th Massachusetts Volunteer Infantry Regiment. Authorized by Secretary of War Edwin Stanton, the 54th was to be formed by the governor of Massachusetts, John A. Andrew, and would fight beneath the flag of that state.

The first officers of the 54th were selected from among the outstanding families in the east. Its leader, Colonel Robert Gould Shaw, was from a family long associated with the abolitionist movement. The lieutenant colonel would be Edward N. Hallowell, the son of a prominent Philadelphia Quaker.

After the first officers were selected, the recruiting began. On February 16, 1863, the following advertisement was placed in the *Boston Journal*:

To Colored Men

Wanted. Good men for the Fifty-fourth Regiment of Massachusetts Volunteers of African descent, Col. Robert G. Shaw. $100 bounty at expiration of term of service. Pay $13 per month, and State aid for families. All necessary information can be obtained at the office, corner Cambridge and North Russell Streets.

Lieut. J.W.M. Appleton
Recruiting Officer

Frederick Douglass and his grandson Joseph. *Library of Congress*

"Who Would Be Free, Themselves Must Strike the Blow!"

$200   **$200**

COLORED MEN
Of Burlington Co.,

Your Country calls you to the Field of Martial Glory. Providence has offered you an opportunity to vindicate the Patriotism and Manhood of your Race. Some of your brothers accepting this offer on many a well-fought field, have written their names on history's immortal page amongst the bravest of the brave.

NOW IS YOUR TIME!

Remember, that every blow you strike at the call of your Government against this accursed Slaveholders' Rebellion, you Break the Shackles from the Limbs of your Kindred and their Wives and Children.

The Board of Freeholders of Burlington Co.

Now offers to every Able-Bodied COLORED MAN who volunteers in the Service of his Country a BOUNTY of

$200   CASH! $200
WHEN SWORN INTO THE SERVICE, and
$10 PER MONTH
WHILE IN SUCH SERVICE.   COME ONE!   COME ALL!

GEO. SNYDER,
Recruiting Agent for Colored Volunteers of Burlington County.

U. S. Steam Print, Ledger Buildings, Philada

Free African leaders took up the appeal. Speeches were made by men such as Martin R. Delaney, Charles L. Redmond, William Wells Brown, Henry Garnet, and Frederick Douglass, whose sons enlisted.

The list of wealthy whites who contributed funds for the raising of the 54th grew each day. The 54th, the first black regiment from the free states, was looked upon by abolitionists as a test of their willingness to fight for their own freedom.

African men came in droves to volunteer. Thousands were interviewed and examined. Men were rejected for the smallest physical deficiency. Only "the best" were wanted.

Robert Forten, grandson of James Forten, came from Europe. Men who had escaped Southern slavery and fled to Canada, such as Joshua Dunbar, returned to the United States to fight. For the most part the men of the 54th had been free before the war. Now they would be fighting for the freedom of their people, and for the extinction of slavery. They knew about the no-quarter policy of the Confederacy, but years of choking back their feelings while loved ones were beaten, years of turning away as other Africans were degraded, had ended. Now they could stand up and fight back! Now was their time to vent the rage of years. Now was the time to either free their race or die trying. Perhaps some of them, as they signed to fight, thought of the old Negro spiritual that had been sung for years at secret plantation meetings:

Recruiting poster. *New York Public Library, Schomburg Collection*

159

Oh, Freedom!

Oh, freedom! Oh, freedom!
Oh, freedom over me!
And before I'd be a slave
I'll be buried in my grave
And go home to my Lord and be free.

No more moaning,
No more moaning,

Facing page, far left: Henry Munroe, 54th Massachusetts Infantry Regiment, Company C. Left: Alexander H. Johnson, 54th. *Massachusetts Historical Society*

This page: John Goosberry, black fifer, 54th. *Massachusetts Historical Society*

No more moaning over me!
And before I'd be a slave
I'll be buried in my grave
And go home to my Lord and be free.

The regiment, trained at Camp Meigs in Readville, Massachusetts, drilled and marched day and night. The men learned how to use their equipment and how to take care of it. They were special, and they knew it. The nation would be watching their

Charles Douglass and Lewis Douglass, the sons of Frederick Douglass. *Moorland-Spingarn Research Center, Howard University*

performance, waiting to see if they were really willing to make the sacrifices required of them. Would these soldiers merely wear the uniform, or were they truly men of war?

On May 18, 1863, their training completed, they were presented with their regimental flags.

On May 28, at six thirty in the morning, the 54th lined up. The day was bright and warm, and the men were ready. Roll call was

162

taken. Each noncommissioned officer reported to the officer in charge of his company. Colonel Shaw received the report and ordered the men brought to attention.

"Forward . . . march!"

The formation started off. The streets were lined with people. Children waved from windows. Flags hung from the balconies. The band struck up the stirring chords of "John Brown's Body" as they marched toward Battery Wharf. The 54th was on its way.

At one o'clock they embarked on the steamer *De Molay*. On board the men relaxed and congratulated each other. Some waved to the crowd still milling about the pier until it dropped from view. The men turned away, many of them caught up in their private thoughts. Others looked out to sea.

While the war had, to a large degree, been romanticized in the South, there were no illusions for the men of the 54th. Not for the African soldiers, nor for their white officers.

It is so often the mothers who are the last influences on the sons who go off to war. J.E.B. Stuart's mother wrote to Robert E. Lee, asking him to accept her son, showing her anxiety that he be involved in the war between the states. Lieutenant John W. M. Appleton was the first white officer recruited for the 54th after Shaw and Hallowell had been selected to lead the regiment. This letter from his mother reflects her concern.

My Dear John,

I wish I could say good bye and impress a kiss on your ever pale cheek. You love your little daughter, my love for my first born son you can never feel, but dear as you are, I can now give you up to God and your country, trusting in his own good time you will be again restored to us in health and peace. Let us hear from you my son whenever you can and think night and morning intercessions will be made for you to Him who heareth prayer.

God help and keep you my good and faithful son. *Mother*

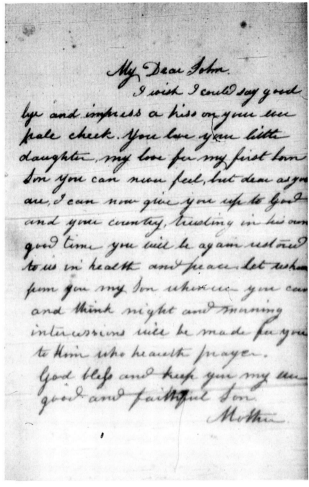

A mother's letter to her son, Lt. John Appleton. *University of West Virginia*

John Appleton. *University of West Virginia*

What this touching letter does not say is that Appleton did not have to fight in the Civil War, nor did he have to fight with the untried United States Colored Troops. During the Civil War Northerners could and often did pay someone to take their place when they were drafted. The Appleton family, however, were

165

noted abolitionists, and it was in this context that John Appleton volunteered to serve with the 54th.

The 54th sailed from Boston to South Carolina. It was Appleton's first trip to the deep South. As the regiment sailed off the
coast of South Carolina, he was struck by its incredible beauty.
We pick up his diary entries:

We ran from side to side of the ship to see the different plantations and
were delighted with this part of the voyage. Beaufort, at which place we
arrived about half past seven o'clock was one of the prettiest and most
picturesque places imaginable.

St. Simon's Island, Georgia
June 9th, 1863

In sight of untamed Rebeldom. We had a rather rough passage last night,
but now we are anchored on St. Simon's Sound with land on both sides
of us. On the right hand St. Simon's Island and on it Butler King's plantations. I have just been on shore with a boat crew to land the Adjutant and
Quartermaster.

It is a very beautiful place but ruined—Oleanders as high as a small
house were covered with red and white flowers, lilies grew in bunches, the
stems as large as my thumb. The flowers very fragrant. Orange trees,
some kind of Palms, tamarinds, Magnolias, and other tropical plants. Gay
birds and butterflies helped to make the pretty scene. Mocking birds
abounded.

But the 54th had not come to South Carolina to see the beautiful sights. They had come to fight. They were in a war. Appleton's diary entries speak of the war. They tell of a soldier who
is executed for desertion, of the burning of mansions and entire

16

Fort Wagner

The plantations along the river had been deserted except for a handful of Africans. Civilians, black and white, eyed the African troops warily. They had never seen black men in uniforms before. Barefoot black boys marched down the street carrying sticks as they imitated the soldiers. For the first time in their lives they had black men to look up to, black men who filled their hearts with pride and marched to the beat of the drums of war.

The business of the 54th was war. There had been brief encounters with Rebel soldiers in a wooded area off the coast. The soldiers had faced the enemy for the first time, and the Rebels had retreated. The Confederates hadn't been defeated; they were merely feeling out the new troops thrown against them by the Union.

cities along the coast. Sometimes the fires were so intense that the Union troops had to shield their faces as they sailed past.

The men were in good spirits and spoiling for a fight. They knew that if Richmond, Virginia, was the head of the Confederacy, then Charleston, South Carolina, was its heart; and now it lay before them, a glittering jewel on the sultry, wind-blown coast, protected only by a fort called Wagner.

Appleton had been told that there were only a few thousand men left to defend Wagner. The Rebels would be outnumbered and outgunned, but nobody expected them to be easy targets.

Appleton read the combat reports eagerly to see how the black men reacted to the fighting. He read that they were doing well. They had fought, had maintained their lines, and had conducted themselves like men of war. The officers of the 54th had been sure that the men would fight, but still it was reassuring to know that the first battles had proved them right. Still, the small forays against a handful of Rebels were not the text of full-fledged battle.

The men of the 54th were no less apprehensive about their officers. Colonel Shaw certainly didn't seem very tough, and Appleton was strangely aloof, almost cold-blooded. Time would tell how these white sons of wealthy New Englanders and the black sons of poor men would fight together.

At Port Royal, South Carolina, a school for the "contraband"—the escaped Africans—was set up. Yankee teachers, white and black, were teaching the newly freed Africans to read and write. In years to come the Port Royal experiment became a model for Reconstruction.

Colonel Robert Gould Shaw was a handsome man, clean shaven, almost regal in bearing. He understood his mission well: to fight for the preservation of the Union. He was comfortable with his officers and yet there was something different about him, an attitude at once heroic and fatalistic.

There were rumors that the 54th would attack Charleston. There were other rumors that they would be rearmed with pikes instead of rifles. In the meantime, like all soldiers before them and since, the 54th endured the endless waiting.

One man had accidentally drowned. Another man deserted and was recaptured. He was asked why he should not be executed. His explanation of his desertion was inadequate, and Appleton noted that he was executed.

Colonel Shaw wanted desperately to know the men he would to lead into battle. He had an idea of who they were, having seen them drill in Massachusetts, watched them on guard duty, and observed them in light skirmishes with the enemy, but it wasn't enough.

One night he attended a religious service, where he saw for the first time the religious fervor of the men he was leading. He saw how they committed themselves completely to what they believed in. On that hot summer night in South Carolina it was the love of God that he was seeing, but Shaw knew it was much more. These men were believers—in God, in life, and in freedom. They were willing to give their lives for what they believed in. Perhaps it was at that time that he began to think he might have to surrender his own life for the cause he believed in.

On July 2, 1863, while having tea with some officers, he met a teacher from Massachusetts. She was charming, gentle, and black. Charlotte Forten, the granddaughter of James Forten

Charlotte Forten, granddaughter of James Forten, who had fought in the Revolutionary War. She taught in the free school for Africans near Fort Wagner during the Civil War. *Moorland-Spingarn Research Center, Howard University*

from Philadelphia, thought the young colonel looked almost "girlish."

Shaw mentioned to her that he didn't understand the "shout," the intensely emotional religious event he had witnessed. Young Charlotte Forten explained that her people were capable of giving themselves up completely to their emotions, that their feelings for their God were so complete that they could express those feelings physically and shout them to the very heavens.

Colonel Shaw knew that he must somehow reach that point, the point at which he could shout his beliefs to the world and fling his body to the heavens.

On July 16, the 54th Massachusetts Volunteer Infantry fought against the Rebel stronghold, helping to push the Rebels back into Fort Wagner and the fortifications surrounding Charleston. Then they regrouped and waited for further orders.

On July 18 the 54th were among the soldiers who would try to take Fort Wagner. It was estimated (wrongly) that there were fewer than two thousand men in the fort. The officers prepared themselves for the battle that was to come. They told each other where on their persons they had letters for their loved ones in the case of their deaths. They reassured each other and said their good-byes. Colonel Shaw, fearing that he would not return from the raid, spoke quietly, almost sadly, as he prepared himself for the assault.

The attack was readied, the men lined up to charge the fort.

Facing page, top: Attack on Fort Wagner. *Harper's Weekly*

Bottom: Black Union troops occupied Fort Wagner when it was abandoned by Confederate troops. *Massachusetts Historical Society*

Appleton tells, in his journal, of Colonel Shaw's review of his troops.

When he came over to our end of the line, he once stood and looked fixedly at me. I was the only officer standing up at the time. It seemed he was about to speak, but did not. He wore a round jacket, with silver eagles pinned on his shoulders. A cap and his short stature and fair hair and face beardless, except for a mustache, made him look very boyish.

. . . Soon the declining day brought the early darkness, and the word came to rise, and forward. We moved at quick time, with fixed bayonets. All the time the guns of the fleet and shore batteries had been thundering away. "Prove yourselves, men," said the colonel as we started. Our lines were about sixteen hundred yards from the fort. As we advanced fire was opened upon us.

. . . The fire became terrible—shell, canister, and musket balls tore through us. Jones' Co., in the second line, which was behind, closed up on us in their excitement, and Willie was busy beating them back. The terrible war deafened us, as we pressed on, at last, we reached the moat of the fort.

The moat, in front of the parapet, was filled with water through which the men had to run, while above them on the parapet the Rebel soldiers fired at the oncoming men. They were defending their fort, their country, their lives.

Once the men of the 54th reached the parapet, they would have to scale it, facing the musket fire at point-blank range, facing the bayonets of the Rebel soldiers.

They ran through the moat, stepping over the bodies of fallen

A page from Appleton's diary, which he illustrated to show the approach to Fort Wagner. *University of West Virginia*

Fort unaided, our duty is to hold what
little we have gained, until the attack
of the Brigade behind us, and to keep
if possible the enemy from firing their
cannon upon our advancing troops. To
that task we bent our energies. Capts
Pope and Jones, and Lieut Emerson, who
had just been assigned to my company,
and myself, with a crowd of our men
of all companies perhaps fifty in
number now commenced firing at every
rebel who showed himself — We picked
up the muskets of the fallen, but found
many ineffective from being filled with
sand. The coolness and bravery of these
officers and men was very marked

The enemy were particularly troublesome
from their bastion on our left, one
man in particular with a broad brimmed hat
hit some one of our men every time he fired
I owned a length

to pick him off, but he could not, so
Capt Pope and I fired at him at
the same time when he next showed
himself, and he disappeared, and we
saw no more of him. A wounded
soldier of my company lay with his
back against the fort, his broken arm
across his body. He was taking cart-
ridges from his box tearing them out
laying them on his wounded arm
for which Emerson, who was doing
good work with a musket. Emerson was
but 17 yrs old and as brave as a
little lion, Most of our officers were

comrades, and started the climb up the steep parapet. Colonel Shaw was with the flag bearer. Appleton could see him on his left. Appleton began the difficult climb up the stone wall, fighting off the men above him trying to push him down to the moat. He wrote in his journal,

On the top of the works we met the Rebels and by the flashes of the guns we looked down into the fort, apparently a sea of bayonets. The colonel planted the colors [flag]. . . ."

Facing page, far left: Sergeant Major John H. Wilson of the 54th. *University of West Virginia.* Left: Sergeant Henry Stewart was active in the recruitment of the 54th. Like a great number of the soldiers on both sides, he died of disease after the battle of Fort Wagner. *Massachusetts Historical Society*

This page: Soldier of the 54th, Charles H. Arnum. *Massachusetts Historical Society*

Colonel Robert Shaw planted the Union flag and was instantly knocked backward as several Rebel shells ripped into him. He fell dead on the wall, the colors waving over him, torn with bullets. Sergeant Carney grabbed it. Bullets whined through the air and men screamed in agony. The 54th was beaten back.

The Rebels, who had been driven off the parapet, now returned with a fury. They swept the 54th off the parapet and down into the moat. The Rebels fought with muskets, knives, clubs, anything they could get their hands on. Draped across the parapet, and on the slope that led to it, were the bodies of the men who had fallen, most of them from the 54th. Dead and wounded Rebels lay among them. At the very bottom of the slope a private seemed to be sitting calmly, his lifeless body almost casual in its attitude.

Appleton was between the slope and the moat. He saw many men about him whom he recognized—nineteen-year-old Colonel Pope, badly wounded; eighteen-year-old Captain Russell, dead.

Appleton tried to prevent the Rebels from manning a gun mounted on the parapet above them. Calmly, he picked off the Rebels rushing to the gun pivot. Sergeant Carney, the standard-bearer, brought the regiment's colors from the parapet.

The 54th retreated to a rise just beyond the moat as the Rebels, their faces illuminated over the flashing muskets, rained down fire upon them. The Confederate soldiers had taken the brunt of the attack and had survived.

The 54th waited for the next brigade to move up and take advantage of the position they had gained, but none appeared. They began the painful retreat.

Fort Wagner was put under siege by Union forces. The Confederate forces held out, with terrible losses, until the first week of September.

But the 54th had proved itself in battle. They had carried the courage of a race through a storm of Confederate bullets and through the terrible burden of their own fear to the very teeth of the enemy.

Many were killed during the attack; others were taken prisoner and survived the war. The remaining men of the 54th continued fighting. When Fort Wagner finally fell, the 54th was one of the first troops to enter the former Confederate stronghold.

The entrance of African troops into the war was another blow to the beleaguered Confederacy. Northern newspapers said that Lee's surrender at Appomattox was hastened by a full year by the entrance of the 180,000 soldiers of African descent.

They fought at Fort Wagner, at Milliken's Bend, at Chafin's Farm, at a hundred other battles throughout the South. Africans on plantations served as spies and scouts for the Union armies. Thousands of Africans served in the Union navy, where they were fully integrated with white soldiers.

The "colored" soldiers also suffered abuse, much of it at the hands of their own Union forces. Sometimes during battles they were not supported by white companies. At other times they were fired upon by Union troops, and more than one Union commander sent them out into open fields to draw fire to reveal enemy positions.

The War Between the States was one of the cruellest in American history. Southern homes were routinely looted, Southern troops often killed rather than captured. Part of the reason for the abuse was the lack of preparation to care for prisoners: Over 60,000 Union soldiers died in Southern prison camps and at least half that many Confederates died in Union hands.

The most notable abuse against African soldiers was at Fort Pillow, Arkansas. The Confederates, under the leadership of Nathan B. Forrest, a slave dealer from Memphis, demanded surrender of the fort, which was held by Northern troops. Forrest sent a message to the Union commander stating that if the fort surrendered, he would treat the whites as prisoners of war and simply return the Africans to their masters. If it did not surrender at once, he would follow Confederate policy and give the Africans no quarter.

The Union forces did not surrender, and the Confederates took the fort after a brief battle. Many African soldiers, and some whites, were slaughtered.

Confederate troops had learned that Africans, given a chance to fight for their freedom, were not the docile, fearful people they had held on their plantations. At Pocotaligo Bridge in South Carolina, a Confederate force attacking Union forces sent packs of bloodhounds against black soldiers of the 1st South Carolina Regiment (Colored). Before the war these bloodhounds had been used to track down runaway blacks. The African soldiers killed the dogs quickly and then went calmly about the business of repelling the Confederate charge.

By the end of the war 180,000 African men were fighting for the Union cause. Another 200,000 served in service units as teamsters, laborers, dock workers, and guides. Sergeant William H. Carney of the 54th was one of twenty-three Africans to win the Congressional Medal of Honor for bravery during the war. African women served as laborers, nurses, spies, and guides.

The Africans proved beyond a doubt their courage, their fighting ability, and their determination to be free.

17

The First Taste of Freedom

On April 9, 1865, General Robert E. Lee surrendered at Appomattox, Virginia, to General Ulysses S. Grant. Several of the Dandridge boys were there, and so were hundreds of Union soldiers, including the 45th Colored Regiment from West Virginia. For all practical purposes the War of the Rebellion was over. There was still sporadic fighting in the deep South; some Confederate soldiers left for South America rather than surrender to the North.

The South was in shambles, with many of its largest cities left in ruins. The soldiers of the Confederate army drifted back to farms and cities to find a crushed economy, their homes destroyed, their loved ones demoralized.

At The Bower in Jefferson County, West Virginia, the Dandridges were no longer the wealthy family they had been before the war, when they could have mortgaged their Africans or sold them to pay off their debts. Now the Africans were free. John Pendleton Kennedy received a letter from Philip Dandridge describing what had happened to his brother, Stephen.

With all his once fine estate, Stephen Dandridge has so little with which to feed and clothe him, that I have not the heart to take anything from him, beyond what he may think proper to offer. . . . I wonder if our friend and kinsman, who has many most excellent qualities, has not by this time some perception that he is one of these dupes and victims. . . .

—*John Pendleton Kennedy from Baltimore* by Charles H. Bohner

In the North there was triumph. Victory overshadowed the specter of maimed and injured men returning from a war that few understood.

For Africans, many of whom lived in the South, it was a time of joy and of confusion. Most of them did not have homes to return to, nor employment as free men. Those who had remained on the plantations during the war were suddenly free, but without the knowledge or skills to survive in the competitive system in which they found themselves. What did it mean to be free in the United States? Most of the newly freed Africans did not know.

The celebrations in the North did not last long. On April 14, 1865, President Abraham Lincoln and his wife attended a play, *Our American Cousin*, at Ford's Theater in Washington. As they sat in the box, an actor named John Wilkes Booth crept quietly in behind them. He raised his pistol and fatally wounded the sixteenth president of the United States.

The nation mourned. Lincoln had been assassinated at a time when the divided nation desperately needed someone who could heal it.

To many Southern whites the freedom of the Africans was both a challenge and a reminder of the war they had just lost. The Africans had fought against them. Those who had fought, many of whom still lived in the South, were part of the conquering army. When some Southern states tried to reinstate slavery, Congress responded quickly.

In December 1865 the Thirteenth Amendment was passed.

Neither slavery nor involuntary servitude, except as a punishment for crime whereof the party shall have been duly convicted, shall exist with the United States or any place subject to their jurisdiction.

The nation was in crisis. The South was bloodied and bowed. Southern whites were burdened with a failed economic system and an untried social structure.

There were two schools of thought in the North at the end of the war. One held that the country should be brought back together with as little friction as possible. The second felt that the South should be punished for its role in the war.

In the months following the end of the war most of the policy regarding the South was carried out by soldiers in the field. The Army of the United States of America became, in effect, an army of occupation in the South.

Many Africans drifted back to the plantations and worked in

conditions very close to slavery. Some refused to work at all as they tried to understand what freedom meant. Others, who had done skilled work prior to the war, began to do well almost at once.

From this turmoil two questions arose. What was to become of the South? And what would be the role of the African? From Congress, now completely dominated by Northern politicians, came the plan that would be known as Reconstruction.

The first function of Reconstruction was to maintain order. The Union Army protected the rights of the newly freed Africans, while the Freedmen's Bureau, a government agency, was established to ease the transition of the Africans from captivity to freedom. It was designed to regulate the relationships between the Africans and Southern whites.

But while the Freedmen's Bureau did offer physical protection for the newly freed Africans, its basic approach was still that of a conquering army. Laws were passed denying the right to vote to anyone who had participated in the war on the side of the Confederacy. Union officers created an order that made sure that the South was "punished." In disputes between whites and blacks the Union officers most often sided with the blacks. Some Southern plantations were broken up and given or sold cheaply to blacks. Blacks were voted into Southern legislatures. Many of the Africans so elected, in light of previous laws against educating blacks, were surprisingly capable; others were less so.

There would later be a general amnesty, an act allowing all citizens the right to vote. But the bitterness of Reconstruction did nothing to foster workable relationships between the races.

Southern whites, who had banded together to form a separate country during the war, now banded together racially.

The problems of the South were not addressed, and would not be for years to come. The opportunity to build the South into an economically viable section of the country, and at the same time to help the newly freed Africans, was lost as Northern politicians, who first thought of punishing the Rebels, returned to their usual fare of sectional interests.

Perhaps the one clearly successful aspect of Reconstruction was the establishment of schools and colleges for Africans. Although the Freedmen's Bureau did offer encouragement to these schools, for the most part it was individuals and Northern religious groups who made the real difference. Howard University in Washington, D.C., was founded and supported in large part by General Oliver Otis Howard of the Union Army. General Samuel Chapman Armstrong was the founder and first commander of Hampton Normal and Industrial Institute, later Hampton University, in Virginia. Various Protestant groups sent teachers and donations of books and money. One of these groups was the American Baptist Home Mission Society.

———————

The American Baptist Home Mission Society had long been an advocate of total abolition and for decades before the war had preached the evils of slavery. When the war was over, the Baptists decided to render service to the Africans by building schools and churches in the South. Due to their influence, such schools as Arkansas Baptist, Bishop College, Morehouse College,

185

Sherman and his generals. The general with one arm is Oliver Otis Howard, after whom Howard University is named. *Library of Congress*

Shaw University, Spelman College, and Virginia Union, among others, were created. A great deal of the Baptists' work was done by women. One of them was Anne S. Dudley.

Anne S. Dudley was graduated from the Seminary Department of Bates College in Maine, and in 1865 she came to the

Anne S. Dudley. My family attended the church in Martinsburg that she founded. *American Baptist Association*

Shenandoah Valley to work among the freedmen.

The first school for Africans in the upper valley was set up at Harpers Ferry, West Virginia. The school was attended at first by nineteen poorly dressed, poorly disciplined young children desperately needing the basic skills of reading, writing, and arithmetic. The children had never held a book before, had never been inside a classroom. White opposition to the school was immediate, and often violent. Teachers were hooted at and sometimes stoned as they went about town. They slept on floors and in the homes of friends. Often there wasn't enough to eat, and there were never enough supplies. This report in *The Missionary Helper*, a periodical published by the Freewill Baptists, describes the scene:

Jan. 2, 1867, the first Free Baptist church was organized in the Shenandoah Valley at Martinsburg. One never to be forgotten morning a few months later the Lord said to me, "Arise and build." I took the message joyfully and told the people I was sure if we did our best the Lord would supply all needed help. The colored people were living in log-cabins, cellar-kitchens, poor, with small wages. Looking on the human side it seemed certainly impossible to accomplish such a task, as all building material was at that time very expensive. On the heavenward side all as bright as the noonday sun. At Christmas we had $60.

I was teaching in an old log-barn, with a row of shelves around the walls for writing, benches without backs, boards for extra seats, as long as there was room. Day and evening schools and meetings were in constant session, with the single exception of one night in a month. The room was always crowded to its utmost capacity.

In 1867 a philanthropist, John Storer of Phillips, Maine,

promised $10,000—a great deal of money in those days—to expand the school. The Baptists would have to raise a similar amount to receive Storer's grant.

The Freewill Baptist Woman's Missionary Society solicited help from a sympathetic General Howard, collected nickels and

Dudley Baptist Church today. *Author*

dimes from New England children, and begged prominent people throughout the country. Finally the money was raised and Storer College was established.

The Reverend Nathan Cook Brackett was the first head of the small school. He would devote most of the rest of his life to the cause of education for the Africans at Harpers Ferry.

Meanwhile, Anne S. Dudley was about the business of maintaining support for the school and establishing a church in nearby Martinsburg. She was so despised by the local citizens that she would often be deliberately pushed off the sidewalks and into the streets. Finally, everywhere she went several sturdy African men accompanied her as bodyguards. The feisty little woman defied her attackers and continued her efforts to build in Harpers Ferry and Martinsburg. The church, officially known as the Freewill Baptist Church, was known among the local black population as Dudley Baptist.

The school prospered little by little. It was not a "college" in the modern sense of the word, but was devoted to providing the freedmen and women with the basic tools of education. At first it was simply reading and writing, but later Storer became a school that taught young people to become teachers so that they could spread their knowledge.

———————

Facing page, top: Storer College. *Harpers Ferry State Park Archives*
Bottom: Storer College today. *Author*

Students and teachers of early Storer College. *Harpers Ferry State Park Archives*

The Missionary Helper of May 1878 described it this way:

In addition to the number of regular teachers that Storer has sent to the many places, but for them, there would be none to go, there is a class of transient pupils who count the few weeks spent here the happiest of their lives. Inside these walls scores have learned to read and write . . . and to cast off shackles that will never more bind them, for what is more cruel than the bondage of ignorance?

Frederick Douglass, who had once been held in captivity in West Virginia, was interested in the school and delivered a graduation speech, pointing out, among other things, that the college had been established at Harpers Ferry, the site of John Brown's raid on the arsenal years earlier. One of the young women in the first classes at Storer was little Louisa Jackson, who had been only four years old when John Brown raided the arsenal. She would later marry Lucas Dennis, the brother of my great-grandmother Dolly Dennis.

By 1874 David Hunter Strother noted in *Harper's New Monthly Magazine* that the school was like any other he had seen.

The room will accommodate a hundred and thirty pupils, with seats and desks, and in winter is always full to overflowing. In summer the attendance is reduced one half, owing to the necessity of the older pupils going out to service, or engaging in remunerative labor of some sort. The children were of both sexes, ranging from three to twenty years of age, neatly and comfortably clad, well fed, healthy, and cheerful, with an uncommon array of agreeable and intelligent countenances peering over the tops of desks. They were also remarkably docile, orderly, and well mannered, without a trace of the barbaric squalor and rudeness pertaining to the street-corner brat of former days, occasionally found nowadays among those who don't go to school.

The Union Army, which had protected the rights of Africans after the war, discontinued its occupation of the South in 1867. The Freedmen's Bureau stayed in operation for a while longer, but soon it, too, was discontinued. Black people in the South were on their own for the first time.

193

On July 28, 1868, the Fourteenth Amendment to the Constitution established that the Africans, once held in bondage, were officially citizens of the United States. This overturned Justice Roger Taney's opinion, in the Dred Scott Decision, that people of African descent were not and could not be citizens of the United States.

In the months following the end of the War Between the States, Africans—now African Americans—found themselves to be a free people. The chains had been cast off. They had helped to cast them off with their courage, and with their lives. That struggle, the struggle to escape being "owned" by other human beings, had ended. But the struggle to find true equality had just begun.

18

Ida B. Wells

To be free had been the hard thing, to be loosened from the bonds and from the chains, to be away from the whips and the hounds. But there were people who said there was a place for people with black skin and that they had better stay in it. African Americans not content to stay in the places "assigned" them were threatened, intimidated, and sometimes killed. Men who had fought against African-American soldiers in the Civil War and had not defeated them now rode at night to terrorize and shoot from the darkness. But there were people who would stand up to the night riders, who would offer their own definitions of freedom and equality both for themselves and for their people.

What was to be done with the newly freed Africans? Were they to assume equal status with whites in the United States?

What did "equal status" mean? If it meant the right to compete on an equal basis, then the African Americans, most with little or no education and burdened by the racial animosity that characterized their existence in the United States, had little chance. Despite the truly heroic efforts of people like Anne S. Dudley in West Virginia, John S. Fee, founder of Berea College in Kentucky, Generals Oliver Otis Howard in Washington, D.C., and Samuel Chapman Armstrong in Hampton, Virginia, most of the black race in the United States was not doing well.

While the black freedman was struggling for success in the South, so was the poor white. Prior to the war most poor whites had had little chance to succeed in a society of large plantations. Now they had to compete not only with the landowners but also with those Africans who had worked the land. What most Southern whites had at the end of the war was "pride, poverty, and ambition." The North had lost a much smaller percentage of its male population than had the South, and its cities and towns were virtually untouched by the conflicts that had destroyed so much Southern property.

The returning Confederate soldiers found almost no industry and few chances for successful farming. Most of the large plantation owners they might have worked for before the war were in no position to hire them now. In addition they had to face competition for the few chances for employment that did exist.

Africans had been brought to America for one reason: to provide cheap labor. The South was still an agricultural society and still needed that cheap labor. But captive labor could be controlled. Now the African Americans, free from bondage, were competing against whites. But new controls were soon imposed in the form of policies, based solely on race, that restricted opportunities for African Americans.

Naturally these policies met resistance. Laws were passed to overcome this resistance, and when laws failed, some people turned to violence.

The first laws, passed after the Union Army ended its occupation of the South, were known as the Black Codes, and were designed to keep African Americans in an economic and social position below European Americans. The Black Code of Mississippi, for example, said that all "freedmen, free Negroes, or mulattos" who worked for more than a month would have to sign a work contract that was witnessed by either a county officer or two disinterested white persons. A person who subsequently left the job "contracted" for could be forced to return to work. African Americans who could not otherwise support themselves could be forced to "apprentice" themselves to a "competent and suitable person." Further, the Black Code said that African Americans would have to give their former owners first preference to their labor.

Since no one *had* to hire a black person, whites in Mississippi could refuse to give jobs to young blacks; the law would declare them wards of the state and force them to "apprentice" for their former masters. In other words, the laws of Mississippi gave the former owners of Africans the right to reclaim them.

Although there were Black Codes in most areas of the South, they were not enforced everywhere, not even in Mississippi. Most whites accepted the idea that slavery had ended, and even tried to work out relationships between whites and blacks that would help both races.

The Thirteenth Amendment to the U.S. Constitution, abolishing slavery, had been ratified in 1865. The Fourteenth Amendment, giving citizenship to all persons born in the United States or naturalized, was ratified in 1868. The Fifteenth Amendment, which said that no one could be denied the right to vote on account of race, color, or previous condition of servitude, was ratified in 1870. Women continued to be denied the right to vote because of their sex.

Local laws, however, were made to frustrate the efforts of African-American men attempting to vote. Blacks who attempted to vote were often beaten, or their homes were burned. People accused of committing wrongs were executed by mobs, sometimes without trials. The suspected offenses could be anything from murder to disrespect for a white person. The lynchings created an atmosphere of fear in the African-American community. People were afraid to speak up for their rights or to take a stand against injustice. One of the most courageous people in the country at this time was Ida B. Wells.

———————

Ida B. Wells, an African-American woman, was born on July 16, 1862, at the height of the Civil War. In her autobiography, *Crusade for Justice*, she writes:

My father (called Jim) was the son of his master, who owned a plantation in Tippah County, Mississippi, and one of his slave women, Peggy. . . .

My mother was cook to old man Bolling, the contractor and builder to whom my father was apprenticed. She was born in Virginia and was one of ten children. She and two sisters were sold to slave traders when young, and were taken to Mississippi and sold again. . . .

Holly Springs, Mississippi, had missed the worst effects of the war, and when the conflict finally ended, Jim Wells, Ida's father, continued the work he knew best, carpentry. There was plenty of work around Holly Springs, and the growing Wells family did reasonably well. In 1866 the Freedmen's Bureau, in conjunction with the Methodist Church, opened a school nearby; young Ida was sent to it.

"Our job," she wrote later, "was to learn all we could."

Ida's mother went to school with her children, learning to read well enough so that she could read the Bible.

Learning "all we could" came easily to Ida. Her parents, who had never had the opportunity to go to school, encouraged their daughter and were proud of her accomplishments. Although not educated themselves, they understood the power of education and the written word.

Ida went to live for a while with her grandmother in rural Mississippi. It was 1878, the year of a yellow-fever epidemic. Entire communities, especially in the deep South, were coming down with the dreaded disease. Hundreds of people died, and hundreds more fled the disease-infested areas. Among those who died were Jim and Elizabeth Wells.

Ida was devastated. She was warned to stay away from Holly Springs, not even to go back for her parents' funerals. In 1878

African Americans fleeing from yellow fever. *Author*

yellow fever wasn't just a sickness; it was a killer.

But Ida had sisters and brothers in Holly Springs, and she worried about them. She had to do something. She had heard how many people in the little town she had grown up in had already died. She was afraid, but she still took the night train to Holly Springs.

The coach she was riding in was draped in black for two conductors who had died of the fever. The conductor working the train, when he found out where Ida was going, asked her if she hadn't heard about the disease. Ida knew about the fever. It struck hard and quickly. A person feeling well and strong in the morning could be shivering and helpless by the evening.

Sometimes the fever brought on delirium, and the victims would call out to people who weren't there. Sometimes they would just lie in bed, coughing up blood.

"Yes," Ida answered. "I know about the fever."

"Then why in Heaven's name are you going to such a place?" the conductor asked.

"Why are you taking tickets on this train?" she asked.

"Somebody's got to do it" was the uneasy answer.

"That's why I am going home," she said. "I am the oldest of seven living children. There's nobody but me to look after them now. Don't you think I should do my duty, too?"

The conductor didn't answer her.

When Ida arrived home, she found two of the children already ill with the disease, and the youngest child, her brother Stanley, had died. One of her sisters scolded her for taking a chance and returning. Ida looked at her young sister. Stricken with a spinal disorder two years earlier, she couldn't walk normally and could barely drag herself around the small house. Now, in spite of her own affliction and the tragedy that had struck the family, she was trying to be brave. Ida knew, no matter what her sisters said, that they were glad to see her.

With two children ill, Ida couldn't take the family away from home. She would just have to stay and do her best in Holly Springs.

Mercifully the epidemic stopped with the end of summer. The small community of African Americans got together to see what they could do to help what was left of the Wells family.

We have seen that during their years of captivity, African

families were often broken up, and individuals were sold to separate owners. Africans had responded by enlarging the idea of "family" to include people who were not related by blood. When "family" could not mean a common blood, it was extended to mean a common love. In keeping with this tradition, the African-American community of Holly Springs extended their love to the Wells family, deciding that the two youngest girls would join two different families while the two boys would be apprenticed out. A white man who had known and respected the work of Jim Wells agreed to train one of the boys. Eugenie, the girl who was partially paralyzed, would have to be placed in the poorhouse.

But Ida would have none of it. Her parents had taught her that people took care of themselves if they possibly could. Ida was only sixteen. She would take care of herself and her family. She passed the examination for schoolteacher and was offered a job teaching in a small school for "colored" children. The school was six miles away from Holly Springs in a rural area, and she had to ride a mule to get there and back, but it paid twenty-five dollars a month. The parents of the students in the school were so grateful to have a teacher for their children that they often gave her eggs and butter to take home.

Ida's grandmother, already in her seventies, came to live with her and help take care of the children. Ida taught during the week and on weekends did the washing and ironing for the family.

Portrait of Ida B. Wells. *New York Public Library, Schomburg Collection*

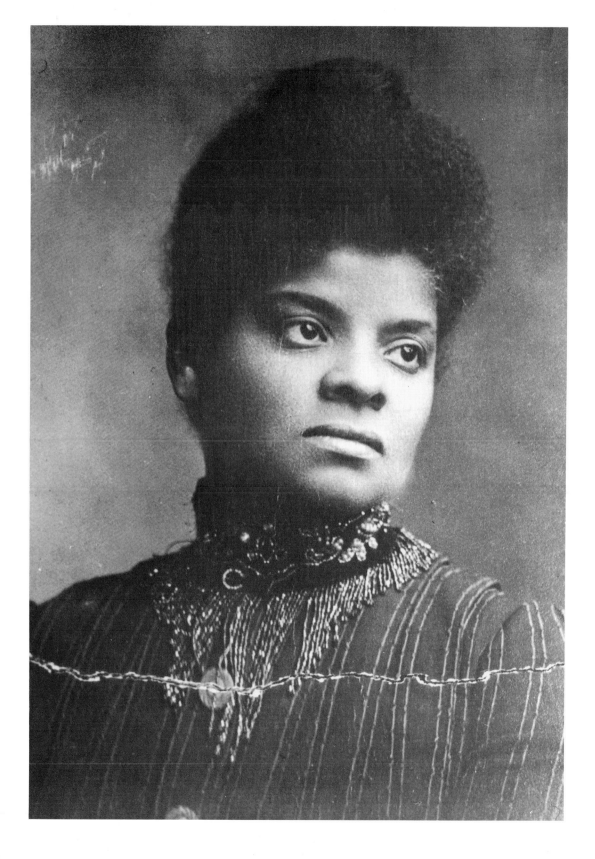

When her grandmother became too ill to care for the smaller children, Ida realized she needed help. She took her sister Eugenie and her two brothers to her aunt's farm in Tennessee, where Eugenie could be cared for and the two boys could help out on the farm. Ida took the two youngest girls with her to Memphis, where she found a teaching job in Shelby County, Tennessee. She also started studying for the teacher's examination in Memphis. If it was possible to better her condition, Ida Wells was going to do it.

By the time that Ida was twenty-two, she was well established as a schoolteacher. She was always conscious of how her people were treated and was dismayed that so many black male leaders seemed willing to tolerate the treatment.

On May 4, 1884, on the way to school, Ida boarded a train and took a seat in the "ladies' coach" of the two-car train. Ida was quietly reading when the white conductor, collecting tickets, told her she would have to move to the other car. The "other car" was the smoker, usually filled with workmen and with bothersome cigar and cigarette smoke. Ida realized that the conductor was telling her to move because of her color. She refused to go.

The conductor decided he would simply move the small, brown-skinned woman out of the car. It was easier said than done. She grabbed onto the railing of the seat in front of her and held on to it as tightly as she could. When the conductor put his hand on hers to pull it off the rail, she sank her teeth into the back of his hand.

The conductor went for help and returned with two more

men. Together they succeeded in dragging her out of the car, much to the delight of the whites who were watching. Ida still refused to go into the smoker: She got off the train.

Ida Wells had been defeated by the sheer strength of three men and she was, indeed, rather small. But the fight was not over yet. She returned to Memphis, contacted a lawyer, and sued the railroad.

After months of delay the case was finally tried before a judge who had been a Union soldier in the war. Ida presented her own case and won. The *Memphis Daily Appeal* in big headlines called Ida "A Darky Damsel."

The railroad appealed the case to the state Supreme Court, where the verdict was reversed.

In the end Ida had lost her battle with the railroad, but that didn't mean that she would stop fighting against injustice.

She continued to teach at the country school outside Memphis, coming home only on weekends. During the week, when she wasn't teaching, she would read. She read everything she could get her hands on, from the novels of Charles Dickens, Louisa May Alcott, and Charlotte Brontë to the plays of Shakespeare—and even Oliver Optic's stories for boys.

Coming from a religious family, she also read the Bible. It was through her church activities that her writing career began. Using the pen name Iola, she began writing for a religious publication called *The Evening Star*. Her well-written, lively articles soon attracted the attention of another religious publication, a weekly called *The Living Way*.

It was common practice at the time for newspapers to "bor-

A DARKY DAMSEL

Obtains a Verdict for Damages Against the Chesapeake and Ohio Railroad—What It Cost

To Put a Colored School-Teacher in a Smoking-Car—Verdict for Ida Wells, $500.

Judge Pierce yesterday rendered his decision in the case of Ida Wells vs. the Chesapeake and Ohio railroad. The suit has attracted a good deal of attention, Judge Greer appearing for the plaintiff and Mr. Holmes Cummins for the railroad. From the testimony is appeared that the railroad company had on sale at the time of the grievance of but one kind of passenger tickets, and that plaintiff purchased one good until used from Memp's to Woodstock, paying full price. She took a seat in the ladies' coach, and when approached by the conductor after the train left the depot handed him the ticket. He refused to accept it, and ordered her to go to the other coach, which was similar to that in which she was seated, but which was occupied exclusively by white men and negroes, many of whom were smoking. The plaintiff refused to go, and the conductor, seizing her by the arm, attempted to force her into the other coach. She continued to resist, and was finally put off the train. Judge Pierce rendered the following decision:

Opinion of the Court.

row" articles from one another. Soon the work published with Iola's by-line was being reprinted in a number of African-American newspapers. Ida accepted a part-time job as a regular correspondent, receiving the fancy salary of one dollar a week.

Ida Wells wanted justice for her people and for women. She wasn't willing to take life on anyone else's terms. Freedom, she felt, meant control of one's own life. She fought for that control at every opportunity. In 1889 she was invited to write for a small paper owned by two men in Memphis: *Free Speech and Headlight.* One of the men was the editor, and the other the sales manager. Ida would be the only woman and the only employee without a title. It didn't sound very much like equality to the young woman. With money she had saved, she insisted on buying a share of the paper so that she would be an equal to the men. They agreed to Ida's terms, and Ida, in addition to her teaching, now wrote for the Memphis paper.

Memphis in August can be almost unbearably hot, and the summer of 1892 was no different. Ida was popular in the black community, and she loved the people she worked and lived with. Throughout her life she had been drawn to people who "were doing something for themselves." Three men who met this qualification in Memphis were Thomas Moss, Calvin McDowell, and Henry Stewart. The trio opened The People's Grocery Company, a small store in which they promised to offer good prices and friendly service. Moss was a letter carrier and hoped to work in the store in the evenings. He owned his own home and

News story about the verdict in favor of Ida B. Wells. *Memphis Public Library* had some savings, and he and his wife Betty were close friends of Ida's.

The white owner of the grocery store nearest The People's Grocery Company resented the new store. Soon, after a petty quarrel, it was rumored that some men were going to come and "clean it out."

The owners of The People's Grocery Company posted guards, but at ten o'clock on a Saturday night a group of white men started coming through the rear door of the building that housed the grocery store. Shots rang out and the intruders retreated quickly. Three of them had been wounded.

The next morning the Memphis papers were filled with stories about how several "officers," looking for criminals they believed were hiding in the building, had been fired upon. Tempers heated up. More than a hundred black men were arrested and put in the county jail.

After the War Between the States, several terrorist organizations had been created to "restore white rule" in the South. The most important one of these had been formed in Tennessee: In 1867, under the leadership of former Confederate general Nathan B. Forrest, the Ku Klux Klan had been formed. Forrest had been a slave dealer in Memphis before the war and had been one of the Confederacy's most respected cavalry officers. But even Forrest disliked the excessive violence associated with the Klan. He disbanded the Klan a few years after its formation; but the basic idea under which the Klan operated had taken hold, and new chapters of the Klan opened without Forrest.

African Americans in Memphis feared that if any of the white men injured in the raid died, there would be a lynching. The idea of lynching was simple: A group of people decided that someone should be executed, and acting in conspiracy as if they were judge, jury, and executioner, they proceeded to carry out the killing—usually a hanging—without a trial and with no concern for the legal rights of the person. Sometimes the victim of the lynching had been accused of a crime, but not necessarily. An imagined racial insult would often suffice. Most victims of lynchings were either African Americans or poor whites; lynchers were certain that they would not be punished for their illegal acts.

The Tennessee Rifles, a local black guard unit, kept watch at the jail so that the arrested men could not be taken out and injured. They watched for two days. On Tuesday the papers announced that all the wounded men would recover.

That night the Tennessee Rifles, in an effort to ease the tensions that gripped the town, stayed away from the jail. The morning papers told the story of what happened after they left:

It is said that Tom Moss begged for his life for the sake of his wife and his unborn baby.

The three men had been taken from their cells and killed during the night. The newspapers, unashamedly, reported the murders in gory detail in the morning. Mobs of whites raided and took groceries and whatever else they wanted from The People's Grocery Company. Armed whites shot at protesting African Americans.

Black men had dared to compete with whites in business and had paid for their ambition with their lives. Ida Wells, deeply moved, wrote a passionate editorial in *Free Speech*.

The city of Memphis has demonstrated that neither character nor standing avails the Negro if he dares to protect himself against the white man or becomes his rival. There is nothing we can do about the lynching now, as we are outnumbered and without arms. The white mob could help itself to ammunition without pay, but the order was rigidly enforced against the selling of guns to Negroes. There is therefore only one thing left that we can do; save our money and leave a town which will neither protect our lives and property, nor give us a fair trial in the courts, but takes us out and murders us in cold blood when accused by white persons.

From the time the first records were kept, in 1882, until the last lynchings were recorded in 1968, 4,743 people have been listed as victims of lynching. Of these, 3,446 were African Americans. The lynchings were generally approved both in the South and in the North; some New York papers were to approve of the practice as late as 1945.

The African Americans in Memphis knew that the murder of the three young men was not about punishment for crimes—it was about economic competition. African Americans were supposed to be cheap labor, not businesspeople.

Ida Wells told people to leave Memphis, and they left in droves. Many headed west toward Oklahoma. They went by train, by wagon—and some started out on foot. If Memphis wouldn't allow them to live free and compete fairly, they would find a place that would. Those people who did not leave Memphis stopped buying in white-owned stores and stopped riding the streetcars.

Memphis newspapers, which only six weeks earlier had proudly announced the murder of the three grocery store owners, now tried to discourage blacks from leaving. Memphis businesses suffered with the loss of black patrons, and the streetcar managers came to Ida Wells's paper and asked her to encourage African Americans to ride the streetcars again. Ida was furious at their request, and adamantly refused.

In May 1892 Wells took a trip to cover a religious conference in Philadelphia; from there she went to a meeting in Jersey City, New Jersey, with T. Thomas Fortune, a famous black journalist. He showed her a story in *The New York Sun* that said that a "committee of leading citizens" had gone to the office of the *Free Speech* in Memphis, destroyed the typesetting equipment and the furnishings, and run the business manager out of town. A note had been left saying that anyone who tried to publish the paper in the future would be "punished by death."

Ida Wells was shocked and hurt. It seemed that the racists who wanted to keep her quiet always had the upper hand. When she recovered her composure, she immediately contacted Memphis to see if her business partners were all right. Then she turned her attention to what she would do next. She knew that she wouldn't give up that easily.

T. Thomas Fortune and Jerome B. Peterson, owners and editors of the *New York Age*, gave Wells a partnership in their paper in return for her list of subscribers. Again she was insisting on an equal footing with the two top African-American newspapermen in the country.

Wells immediately began to attack what she saw as the leading problem for African-American people in the United States: the lynchings.

The crusade against lynching in the *New York Age* was a daring act of rebellion against the injustices suffered by African Americans. In the South, blacks' public objections to lynchings nearly always brought quick reprisals. Many Northern black leaders, hoping to balance their positions as leaders of their own people with acceptance by whites, often restricted their protests to those cases in which the victim of the lynching was clearly innocent. They had, in effect, accepted a lower standard of justice for African Americans than for whites, allowing the mobs to pronounce the victims of mob violence guilty until proven innocent. This lack of outrage, not only by some African Americans but by all Americans, was well noted by Ida Wells in a letter to the English paper *Birmingham Daily Post* in May 1893.

In the past ten years over a thousand black men and women and children have met this violent death at the hands of a white mob. And the rest of America has remained silent. Not even when three men were burned alive in the past twelve months, has she opened her mouth to protest against this barbarism.

Ida Wells married an attorney, F. L. Barnett, in 1895, settled in Chicago, and for a while slowed her activism and raised her family. She continued her writing, however, and organized local women's clubs.

In 1921 a group of African-American farmers in Elaine, Arkansas, were offered a price for their cotton that was below that offered to whites. The farmers, who had formed an organization among themselves, refused to sell for the lower price. They were attacked by angry whites who did not want them to compete against white farmers. The black farmers had guns and protected themselves against the attacking mob. A large number of blacks were killed during the riot. Twelve black farmers were rounded up and put into jail. They were beaten and tortured as the local law officials tried to force them to admit to a conspiracy to kill white people.

An all-white jury took only six minutes to convict the twelve men. They were sentenced to death by electrocution. The National Association for the Advancement of Colored People, which had been formed in 1912, sent a telegram to the governor of Arkansas protesting the trial and the sentence. Another telegram of protest was sent by the National Equal Rights League. They were both ignored.

Few people at that time understood that racism was not about white people liking or not liking black people. It was about controlling the economics of the country by keeping blacks dependent on whites. Ida Wells, then almost sixty years old, was president of the Negro Fellowship League. She sent a telegram to the governor of Arkansas stating that if the farmers were executed, her organization would encourage thousands of black people to leave the state. Arkansas, like most other Southern states, was still dependent on cheap black labor. Perhaps recalling what Wells had accomplished in Memphis, perhaps nervous about the national attention that was suddenly being paid to his state, Governor Brough arranged for the farmers to have a new trial.

By now well known in the South for her fight against lynching, Ida Wells visited the men in prison using an assumed name. She asked them to tell her their stories, which they did while a guard sat some fifty feet away reading the Sunday paper. Back in Chicago she published their stories and laid out the facts for the world to see.

Within the year the farmers were free.

While lynchings were opposed by fair-minded people in the South as well as in the North, the mob violence was also condoned by many people from both areas. How many more would have lost their lives to murder by mobs without the work of Ida Wells is difficult to say.

When Ida Wells was sixteen she took on the responsibility of caring for her family, to be both mother and father to her younger siblings because it needed to be done. When she was twenty-two she took on the battle against the Chesapeake & Ohio Railroad because that, too, needed to be done. In Memphis she crusaded against the lynchers of African-American men because it needed to be done. Now, writing for the *New York Age*, she took on lynching across the country. It was Ida Wells who delivered the message that black men and black women were as deserving of justice as whites.

This small woman, armed only with a keen mind and dauntless courage, did more to curtail the practice of lynching than any other person. The battle for African-American rights had moved from the battlefields of the war to the newspapers and the personal courage of people like Ida Wells. Ida B. Wells died in 1931, but the work of this remarkable American heroine will live forever.

19

Lewis Howard Latimer

There are people whose acts, like those of Nat Turner and the soldiers of the 54th Massachusetts Volunteers, catch the fire of the moment and streak like meteors across the face of history, leaving bright records of their accomplishments and undeniable evidence of their stature. There are others whose feats are less spectacular, but whose deeds, when understood, are so important that we must search out their stories and celebrate their lives. Such a man was Lewis Howard Latimer.

Plantation owners and proslavery people offered, as justification for their peculiar institution, the rationalization that Africans were incapable of fending for themselves and needed white supervision and care. It was up to African Americans, free for the first time, to show that indeed they could not only survive, but do as well as white Americans.

What the free African Americans did was to show that they could and would make unique contributions to American life. Scott Joplin, born in Texarkana, Texas, invented ragtime. Madame C. J. Walker was one of the first American women to earn a million dollars. George Washington Carver, born in captivity, made great contributions to the agricultural rebirth of the South. Norbert Rillieux revolutionized the sugar-refining industry with his invention of the vacuum evaporation process, and Garrett A. Morgan invented a gas mask and an automatic stoplight that he later sold to General Electric.

Just as Africans before them had exposed the lies that the captives were content and could not learn to read and write, these men and women exposed as lies the idea that African Americans were not capable of being highly educated or creative. Lewis H. Latimer, by any standard, was an exceptional man who lived through a vital period of history.

———————

Lewis Howard Latimer was born on September 4, 1848, in Chelsea, Massachusetts. It was his father, George Latimer, who had escaped from Norfolk years earlier by stowing away with his wife on a ship headed toward Boston. As a young boy Lewis sold *The Liberator*, the paper published by the white abolitionist William Lloyd Garrison. The young Latimer had read the works of other abolitionists, men such as Lewis Hayden and Frederick Douglass, as well.

Besides selling papers, Lewis worked for his father as a painter and plasterer. As a boy he was quiet, spending long hours by himself reading anything he could get his hands on. He began to write—sometimes carefully worded essays like the ones he read in the *Liberator*, but more often poetry. Drawing brought him a great deal of pleasure. He dreamed of someday being able to write for newspapers, and perhaps even to do the illustrations. When the War Between the States started, the African men in the North at first waited patiently to see what the outcome would be. Then, in 1863, when it was decided that Africans would be allowed to join the Union Army, sixteen-year-old Lewis was interested. Small—barely five feet four inches tall—Lewis saw the big, powerful men of the 54th Massachusetts. Lewis decided to join the navy, where he was accepted as a landsman, a general hand on a ship. He was assigned to the U.S.S. *Massasoit*, a side-wheel gunboat.

The Union forces were trying to blockade the James River to prevent the Confederacy from getting supplies into Virginia by ship, and the *Massasoit* was assigned to the blockade force. With Confederate gun batteries on the shore, young Latimer's life was made exciting. A report filed by its commanding officer gives the details:

U.S.S. *Massasoit*
James River, Virginia, January 24, 1865

SIR: I have the honor to submit the following report of the part taken by this vessel in the action of today:

At 9:50 A.M. I received the order to get underway and proceed up the river prepared for action. At 10:08 A.M. was underway, and, passing the U.S.S. *Hunchback*, took station astern of the U.S.S. *Onondaga* and proceeded up within range of the swamp and Howlett house batteries. At 10:12 beat to quarters and prepared the ship for action. At 10:35 opened

The U.S.S. *Massasoit* was the ship on which Lewis Latimer served during the Civil War. *Courtesy of Louis H. Smaus, U.S. Naval Historical Center*

fire upon the swamp and Howlett house batteries. At 11:55 A.M. ceased firing and dropped down below Dutch Gap Canal and went to dinner. At

12:16 P.M. came to anchor off Aiken's Landing astern of the U.S.S. *Onondaga.* Being for the greater part of the time very nearly abreast of the Crow's Nest battery, of which the enemy have very accurate range, we were struck several times by shot and shell, but sustained no serious injury. Too much credit can not be given to the officers and crew for the manner in which they conducted themselves during the action.

It being the first action the crew ever participated in, they deserve special commendation, acting, as they did, like veterans. Our list of wounded amounts to five. For full particulars of wounded and injuries received I would most respectfully refer you to the enclosed reports of the surgeons, chief engineer, boatswain, and carpenter. Injuries in the sailmaker's department are entirely unimportant. At the first start there was a slight difficulty with the engine, which detained us a few moments.

I am, sir, very respectfully, your obedient servant,

G. Watson Sumner
Lieutenant, Commanding pro tem

Latimer was lucky enough to return from the war in good health. What he needed then was a job. He found one in the office of Crosby and Gould, a Boston law office specializing in patents. They were looking for someone who was reliable, and who was bright enough to do the variety of jobs in their office. Latimer, a quiet, studious young man, presented himself well. His reading and writing were quite good, and his ability to draw was a talent the firm might be able to use. They took a chance on him.

As Latimer worked, he kept his eyes open to what was going on in the office. As office boy he did well, but he thought he could also learn to do the careful drawings the firm sent to Washington when they applied for patents on inventions. The men who did the drawings were called draftsmen and used special drafting tools. Lewis didn't earn much, but he managed to save enough to buy a used drafting set. Now the only thing he had to do was to learn how to use it.

If Latimer's life was marked by any one trait, it was his ability to work hard at whatever it was that he wanted to do. He was never easily discouraged. In the evenings, after a full day's work, he practiced using the drawing tools he had bought until he felt he was as good as the regular draftsmen on the job. He asked for a chance to show what he could do.

When a person invents something, he or she goes to a lawyer and starts the process of getting a patent. The patent legally establishes that the person has indeed invented something new, and something worthwhile, to which she or he has the sole rights. The rights to an invention are important; they keep others from stealing it, or using the invention without paying the inventor.

But to get the invention patented, the idea has to be explained carefully in writing, and drawings have to be made that clearly show how the invention works and how it is unique. The drawing has to be absolutely fine in every detail. Latimer's drawings were excellent, and he was promoted to the position of draftsman. He quickly rose to the rank of chief draftsman in the company. Latimer worked on many patent applications, including those of Alexander Graham Bell, the inventor of the telephone.

By the age of twenty-five Latimer had helped to free his people by fighting in the Civil War, had taught himself drafting,

and had established himself in an excellent job. It was, he thought, a good time to marry the young woman he had met, Mary Wilson. It was for her that he wrote the poem "Ebon Venus":

> *Let others boast of maidens fair,*
> *Of eyes of blue and golden hair;*
> *My heart like needles ever true*
> *Turns to the maid of ebon hue.*

Latimer liked to draw, and he combined his drawing ability with the willingness to apply himself as he established himself as one of the finest draftsmen in the country. He believed in himself and in his own mental capacities. He felt that he could do anything that involved just his mind and the willingness to work. As he saw others applying for patents, he wondered if they were really more inventive than he was. Before his twenty-sixth birthday, Latimer received a patent for one of his own inventions—a device that improved the bathroom facilities on trains. Perhaps his hat had been stolen once, for he also received a patent on a hat rack that could prevent hats from being stolen in restaurants.

In 1879 Thomas Alva Edison invented the incandescent light bulb. The light was a marvelous invention, and it fascinated Latimer. Just as he had studied art in his spare time, and later drafting, now he began to study electricity. He read as much as

Lewis H. Latimer. *New York Public Library, Schomburg Collection*

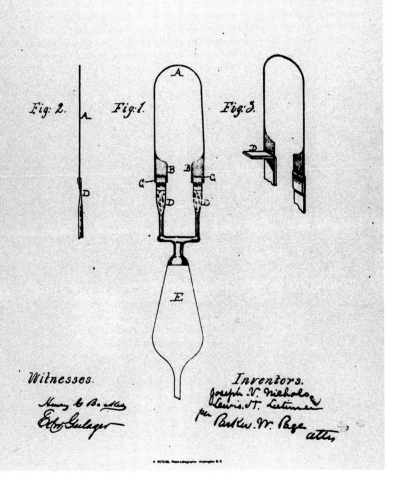

(No Model.)

J. V. NICHOLS & L. H. LATIMER.
ELECTRIC LAMP.

No. 247,097. Patented Sept. 13, 1881.

Fig. 2. Fig. 1. Fig. 3.

Witnesses. Inventors.

One of Latimer's patents. *New York Public Library*

224

he could about the uses of electricity and conducted his own experiments.

His reputation as a draftsman was outstanding, and in 1880 he was hired by Hiram Stevens Maxim, the chief engineer of the United States Electric Lighting Company. Latimer worked as a draftsman for Maxim and continued his own studies of electricity. In 1881 Lewis H. Latimer received a patent for inventing, with Joseph V. Nichols, a way of attaching filaments in lamps. In 1882 he received his most important patent, for an improved process of manufacturing filaments.

Before incandescent lighting most large buildings had gaslights. Gas was piped into the building and regulated by a nozzle. A glass bulb was placed over the nozzle and the gas ignited with a match. Incandescent lighting was safer, cleaner, and much more convenient. The few men who understood this lighting were in high demand. Latimer was an African American who had knowledge and talents that people needed.

The work done by people like Edison, Maxim, and to an extent Latimer changed the way we now live in cities. It was Latimer who helped install the lights in some of the first electrically lighted buildings, such as the old Equitable Building in New York. He also supervised the installation of electric lighting in Philadelphia; London, England; and Montreal, Canada. He learned enough French to speak it to the Canadians. (He was proud of his ability to speak French but was disappointed in his German.)

Lewis Latimer, son of a man held in bondage, was sent by Maxim to England to set up an incandescent-lamp department in Maxim's factory there. Latimer thought he would have little difficulty in England. He was wrong. His English co-workers were not used to taking orders from Americans, especially not black Americans. Eventually, though, they realized that Latimer knew his business, and the department was established. Latimer's ability outweighed all other factors.

It is not unusual for the top experts in any field to work together at some point in their careers. It is no wonder, then, that Latimer would one day work for Thomas Edison. He worked largely in the legal department, as an expert in electricity, using his knowledge of patent law to defend the rights of the Edison company, which had become the General Electric company. In 1918, to further the advances he had already made in the field, Edison put together a band of experts in electricity and electrical lighting called the Edison Pioneers. One of those Pioneers was Lewis H. Latimer.

Lewis Latimer's life was extraordinarily full. He continued to paint, creating many fine portraits of the family he loved, and taught himself to play the flute extremely well. He corresponded with Frederick Douglass, who had met his father, George Latimer, and who admired the son.

He also continued to write poetry. When I visited the home of his granddaughter, Winifred Latimer Norman, she showed me letters indicating that Latimer had received $3.50 for a poem published in the January 24th, 1903, issue of *A Cry for Justice*, but that on November 10, W.E.B. Du Bois had rejected a poem Latimer had submitted to *Crisis* magazine. Even Lewis Latimer was not always successful.

The Edison Pioneers. Edison is in the center, sporting a cane, and Latimer is second from left, front row. *New York Public Library, Schomburg Collection*

In 1906 the Latimers were living in New York and Lewis Latimer was teaching in the evenings at the Henry Street Settlement House. He wrote theatrical comedies and even acted in some of them.

When the nation's major African-American leaders were considering an assembly to assess the direction that African Americans should travel, he was one of those invited. His thinking was appreciated, his importance recognized.

He believed in the arts and conveyed his enthusiasm to his

children. One of his daughters went to Juilliard to study music, the other to Pratt Institute to study art.

He believed in education, whether that education was formal or informal, and he was a friend of Arthur Schomburg, the book lover and collector. He was a lifelong reader.

This quiet man, born in the period when so many of his people were held in degradation—when his own father, anguished and wary of being returned to captivity, was of little comfort to either Lewis or his family—demonstrated that there was genius in that captivity as well as labor.

Lewis H. Latimer died on December 11, 1928, at the age of 80.

Unconquered and Unconquerable
by Lewis H. Latimer

What tho' I suffer through the years
Unnumbered wrongs, unnumbered fears
My soul doth still forbid me tears
Unconquered and unconquerable

What tho' my bed of thorns be made
What tho' my onward cruise be stayed
My soul soars upward undismayed
Unconquered and unconquerable

What tho' by chains confined I lie
What tho' by brutal hands I die
My soul will upward ever fly
Unconquered and unconquerable

I scorn the hand that did me wrong
Tho' suffering days and years be long
My soul still charts that deathless song
Unconquered and unconquerable

20

The Battle in the Courts

The Civil War was over, and African Americans who were the children of people held in slavery were already making contributions to American life. But neither the determination and journalistic skills of an Ida B. Wells nor the creativity of a Lewis H. Latimer gave either of them the same rights that white Americans enjoyed. The United States is a land of laws, and it is those laws that have defined the rights of its citizens. In the Dred Scott case the Supreme Court said that Negroes had no rights because they were not citizens of the United States and therefore could not bring their grievances to the courts. The Fourteenth Amendment to the Constitution declared that all people born in the United States were citizens. This allowed African Americans to use the courts in their attempt to gain equal rights.

The rights of African Americans were denied through *prohibitions* and *inhibitions*. Laws that prevented African Americans from doing certain things, or that made the doing nearly impossible, were prohibitions. For example, a law that said no one could vote if his grandfather did not vote was a prohibition, since the grandfathers of most African Americans had been captives and not allowed to vote.

Other laws prohibited African Americans from eating in certain restaurants, using certain drinking fountains, or being treated in certain hospitals.

Other factors *inhibited* African Americans from exercising their full rights by discouraging them from exercising those rights. The violence against the black farmers in Arkansas, for example, discouraged them from demanding the full price for their crops. Violence against the store owners in Memphis inhibited Africans in that city from owning their own businesses.

One of the first challenges to the laws of prohibition was the case of *Plessy vs. Ferguson.*

At the end of the Civil War a number of so-called "Jim Crow" laws were passed. These laws segregated the races by reserving certain facilities for "whites only" and others for "colored only." It was only a matter of time before black people challenged these laws in court.

In 1892 thousands of African Americans worked in white homes. They prepared food for white families to eat, took care of white babies, and shared bathroom facilities in white homes. But in parts of the country, particularly in the South, they could not drink from the same public water fountains, or eat in the same public restaurants, or ride in the same public railroad cars as whites.

In 1892 an African American named Homer Adolph Plessy, who lived In Louisiana, boarded a train in New Orleans and sat in the section of the train reserved for whites only. He was ordered to leave the car. When he refused, he was arrested. Mr. Plessy admitted that he had violated the state law but claimed that, according to the Constitution, the state had no right to make such a law.

Plessy pointed out that the Thirteenth Amendment says that no person shall be subject to "involuntary servitude" without due process of the law; the Fourteenth Amendment says that "no State shall make or enforce any law which shall abridge the privileges or immunities of citizens of the United States." Plessy argued that the laws of segregation violated these amendments. Ferguson was the name of the lower-court judge who ruled against Plessy.

The case went through the state courts and eventually reached the Supreme Court. People throughout the country followed the case closely. If the Supreme Court said that Louisiana's laws were illegal, all public facilities would be open to all people regardless of color. In 1896 the Supreme Court decided against Plessy, and by doing so decided against all African Americans.

The Court said that the Constitution referred to "political" equality. Separating whites and blacks, the majority opinion said, was a "social" matter, and merely recognized the differences between the races.

Justice Henry B. Brown spoke for the majority:

We consider the underlying fallacy of the plaintiff's argument to consist in the assumption that the enforced separation of the two races stamps the colored race with a badge of inferiority. If this be so, it is not by reason of anything found in the act, but solely because the colored race chooses to put that construction upon it.

Not all the Justices of the Court agreed. Justice John M. Harlan spoke for those who dissented:

What can more certainly arouse race hate, what more certainly create and perpetuate a feeling of distrust between these races, than state enactments, which, in fact, proceed on the ground that colored citizens are so inferior and degraded that they cannot be allowed to sit in public coaches occupied by white citizens? That, as all will admit, is the real meaning of such legislation as was enacted in Louisiana.

The majority opinion stated was that there was a "natural order" of things in which people felt a need to be separated by race. It did not imply, according to the decision of the court, anything other than a desire to be separate. As long as the facilities were "equal," they did not violate the meaning and intent of the Constitution.

The *Plessy vs. Ferguson* decision formed the basis of the "separate but equal" doctrine. This idea of separate public facilities was maintained in the South for the next seventy years. It would one day be the rallying point around which a new struggle would form, the modern civil rights struggle.

233

After *Plessy vs. Ferguson* blacks and whites continued many of the relationships they had known before. Black women still worked in white homes, cooking for white families and cleaning their houses. They still took care of white children.

But the legalized separate facilities, as Justice Harlan had suggested, put the mark of inferiority on blacks. Nothing was so painful as to be told that you couldn't get a glass of water at a counter in a five-and-dime store because of the color of your skin, or you couldn't sit in a waiting room in a bus station with white people. It wasn't so much that the "equal" facilities were usually far from equal; it was the fact that African Americans were being told, from the time they were old enough to understand, that they weren't as good as whites.

What's more, the "separate but equal" doctrine was used to deny African Americans access to educational opportunities, medical services, even seats in movies for years to come. It was a constant reminder that in the United States, the land of their birth, the land that many had died to defend over the years, they would not be treated as equals.

21

Meta Vaux Warrick

William Edward Burghardt Du Bois, the African-American author, editor, and educator, noted that after the Civil War people of African descent were often caught in a dilemma: On the one hand they were Americans, with the same ideas, ambitions, and dreams as other Americans; on the other hand they were trapped in an ethnic identity by American racial attitudes. African Americans could be as gifted, as accomplished, and as wealthy as their white neighbors but found that they would still be regarded differently, would often be judged not by their talents but by color.

The problem was in the minds and hearts of those who were willing to reduce the human adventure to something as superficial as skin color. The answer for African Americans was not to deny their heritage but to embrace it, and in so doing to discover those unique qualities of the black experience that define it as the rich and vital cultural substance from which can grow all the possibilities of life.

William Warrick wasn't worried about supporting a third child. The Warricks owned a catering business and a hair dressing salon, and had made money in real estate. African Americans had lived in freedom in Philadelphia since colonial times, when James Forten had made a fortune manufacturing sails. Black abolitionists, clergyman, political leaders, and businessmen had made the city the most important one for African Americans in the United States. There were many middle-class and upper-middle-class African-American families living in and around Philadelphia when Meta Vaux Warrick was born on June 6, 1877.

Meta was different from most children in America, white or black, in that her family could afford to give her almost anything she wanted. The children she played with most as a young girl were the sons and daughters of prominent merchants. She went to private schools and was trained to be a "lady" as well as to read and write well. Both white and black children attended the schools, and Meta liked being with all of them.

Meta was closer to her father than to her older sister and brother, and William Warrick enjoyed taking his daughter to museums, to the ballet, and for long walks through Philadelphia's Fairmount Park. Meta's ideas of what she wanted to do with her life were influenced to a great extent by her father's love of culture. Like many children, after seeing a ballet she wanted to be a dancer, and she persuaded her family to give her dancing lessons.

The "big-footed fairy" was what her brother, William, called her as she danced from room to room of their large home. Meta ignored her older brother. She didn't mind his racing up and down the block practicing for his track team, she thought, so why should he mind her dancing? She was interested in what her sister, Blanche, was doing with charcoals and paints. There was always an extra piece of paper about that she could draw on, and she did whenever she had a chance.

The Warricks expected their son to go to college. The girls, they thought, would help their mother in the beauty salon. When Meta was ten, she saw that Blanche was already helping her mother wash and set the hair of the women who came to their salon. Meta didn't have any interest in being a hairdresser or in shaping anyone's nails.

Meta enjoyed growing up in Philadelphia. She liked the fancy parties that her parents gave and the elegantly dressed people who came to them. She knew that her family was doing well and that life was clearly more comfortable for them than for many other African Americans she saw.

The Warricks had white friends as well as black, and many of Meta's playmates were white. It was with some of her white girl friends that Meta experienced racism for the first time. A carousel was brought to one of the parks in Philadelphia. It was a small carousel, with brightly colored horses that went up and down on gold and silver bars as it turned to a merry tune.

When the owner said she couldn't ride on the carousel because she was black, she walked away and sat on a bench until her friends returned. She tried not to think about the incident, but in years to come just the sound of the melody she heard that day would upset her.

William Warrick had met a young black painter, Henry Ossawa Tanner, whose work he liked, and had invited him to his home. Tanner, known for his delicate treatment of light, was born in Pittsburgh in 1859 and was the best-known African-American artist in the world at the time. Warrick took Meta to see some of Tanner's work, which was on display at the Philadelphia Academy of Fine Arts.

In her last year of high school Meta won a scholarship to the Pennsylvania School of Industrial Art in Philadelphia. The honor of the scholarship was recognized with pride among her family's friends. Now, the Warrick family knew that they had reached their comfortable position through hard work. William Warrick was a man who sometimes worked twelve to fourteen hours a day and had little patience with those who did not work hard. He didn't consider art a way of making a living, especially for a woman, but he consented to allow Meta to attend art school.

Meta began both to study art and to help in the family businesses. Her teachers at the School of Industrial Art recognized her talent, and by the time she was graduated, she had won several honors.

She continued to paint and experiment with sculpture and read about art. What she read convinced her that if she were to advance in art, it would have to be in Paris.

Most African Americans couldn't afford a trip across the country, and here Meta wanted to go clear across the Atlantic to Paris. There was a difficult decision to be made in the Warrick household.

Meta had the same problem that any other young woman at the time would have had: She needed to convince her parents that they should invest in her study in Paris when neither of them could see how she could use her art to make a living. An aunt spoke up for Meta. She would be delighted to sponsor the girl's studies. After all, that other African-American painter, Tanner, had gone to Paris, and they hadn't heard anything bad about him. If Meta thought her future lay in art, then she was entitled to the chance.

Meta Vaux Warrick was twenty-two when she left for France on the ship *Belgianland* in October 1899. Arriving in Calais, she was tired from the long trip across the ocean but still checked each bag as it was put into the taxi for the train station. There was a short wait for the train, but she was soon settled into a compartment and was absolutely delighted as the train to Paris pulled out of the busy station on schedule.

When Tanner didn't show up at the train station, she picked herself up and went as planned to the American Girls' Club by taxi. The American manager of the club was shocked to see that Meta was an African American. Her letters had been well composed and her references excellent. The manager had expected her to be white.

The manager explained to Meta that she had nothing against her personally, it was just that her presence might offend the

other girls staying at the club or their parents. She refused to let her stay.

Meta was crushed. She had come to Paris filled with excitement and the dreams of an art career. Her first experience there was tainted with the racism she thought she had left behind.

Tanner, having missed Meta at the train station, hurried to the American Girls' Club, where he found her in heated discussion with the manager. He wasn't surprised to find out that she wasn't welcome at the American Girls' Club. The manager and Tanner began looking for other living arrangements for Meta.

Paris was an exciting place for the young American. Monet, Toulouse-Lautrec, and Cézanne were all working or exhibiting their works in Paris. Young artists such as Picasso, Braque, and Utrillo were discussing their works in the bistros. Once she reached the art community, Meta experienced almost no racial prejudice.

She studied drawing techniques in the formal, classical manner, even though she felt her interests going more and more toward sculpture. On her own she worked on sculpture.

In Paris she met some other African Americans as well as Parisians. She attended the Paris Exposition in 1900 as the guest of W.E.B. Du Bois, who at the time was just beginning to discuss the idea that all people of African descent should identify themselves as one people instead of as different African nationalities. Meta was impressed with Du Bois and his philosophy, and started looking more toward African subject matter for her art.

Meta Vaux Warrick, from a solidly middle-class family. *Solomon C. Fuller*

During her last year in Paris, Meta Vaux Warrick had the opportunity to meet Auguste Rodin, already recognized as one of the greatest sculptors of all time. His works, from the familiar *The Thinker* to his larger, more powerful pieces, were known throughout the world. Meta was nervous as she approached Rodin's studio. But the master sculptor greeted her warmly and carefully examined her sketches and the plaster forms she had brought with her. He was impressed with her talents but wondered why she had not chosen more pleasant subjects.

Warrick explained to Rodin that she did not deliberately choose unattractive subjects, although the piece that had impressed Rodin the most, *A Man Eating His Heart Out*, was certainly not a happy one. She sculpted, she said, what captured her imagination at the moment.

Rodin admired the power in Meta's work, told her so, and encouraged her to use his name as a reference. Rodin, whose own pieces were monuments of power, showed Meta some of his work and some of the anatomical studies he was working on.

Meeting Rodin, having him discuss her work and call her a "true sculptor," reinforced Meta's confidence in her art. Art dealers, partly because of Rodin's praise for the young sculptor, began to take note of Meta Warrick's work. It wasn't long before her work was selling in L'Art Nouveau, one of the best of the Paris galleries.

When Meta Warrick finished her studies, she had to decide whether to stay in France or return to the United States. In 1902 she returned to Philadelphia.

In Paris her talents had been celebrated; her work had been

accepted by the European art community and so had she. She was recognized as a very talented sculptor without regard to her color. Her work was good, and people accepted her for that work.

In the United States things were different. African-American artists were often discouraged from entering competitions, and few galleries would display their work. Meta Warrick found she was being rejected because she was black.

Meta Warrick had been raised by her parents in Philadelphia to be "different." An African American who was well educated in a time when few of her people had the opportunity to go to any school, she had traveled and studied in Paris. She was determined to be an artist at a time when most women of color were working as domestics or service workers. The response to her in Philadelphia made her color assume an importance that diminished her talent.

More and more she turned to sculpture to express her pain. She depicted an African slave ship on the way to America, showing the Africans crowded belowdecks. *Mary Turner (A Silent Protest Against Mob Violence)*, done in plaster, was painted after the lynching of several African Americans, among them the woman Mary Turner.

Art critic David Driskell said about her work:

[She] introduced America to the power of Black American and African subjects long before the Harlem Renaissance was under way. Until Meta Warrick, the esthetics of the Black visual artist seemed inextricably tied to the taste of White America. . . . At a time when Picasso and followers of the modernist tradition gleaned design elements from the art of non-Western societies without being responsible for the cultural context out of which the work came, [her] art evidenced a hereditary union between Black Africa and Black America.

One of her most effective pieces is *Talking Skull*, a bronze statue of an African boy communicating with a skull, making a connection between his present and the past.

While visiting a hospital in Massachusetts, Meta Vaux Warrick met Dr. Solomon C. Fuller. As she commented in her notes:

He says he fell in love with me at that visit at Westboro State Hospital. That's what he claims. I had a mass of hair, then. I wouldn't call him a handsome man. Depends on what you call handsome. He was fairly tall and thin.

Solomon proposed, and after some thought Meta accepted. Dr. Fuller started building a home in Framingham, Massachusetts.

The neighbors didn't learn that the doctor was black until the builders had started the excavation for the cellar. Then they circulated a petition to keep him out of the neighborhood. A friend offered them a lot in another area, but Meta would have none of it. She insisted on not giving in to the neighbors. The house went up slowly, but it went up where Meta wanted it.

He didn't carry me across the threshold. That was too folderol for him. I had to walk!

Solomon C. Fuller was born in Monrovia, Liberia, on August 11, 1872. Earlier we read that his grandfather, John Lewis Ful-

Talking Skull by Meta Warrick. *Solomon C. Fuller*

ler, and his father, Solomon—then sixteen—had emigrated to Liberia from Norfolk, Virginia, a decade before the Civil War. John Fuller, born into captivity in Petersburg, Virginia, had been a highly skilled boot- and shoemaker. His skills were such that he was able to strike a deal with the man who held him to keep part of his earnings. Fuller saved enough money to buy his own freedom and that of a white indentured servant named Nancy who later became his wife.

The Fuller family prospered in Liberia, growing coffee for export and serving as government officials. When Solomon C. Fuller—the son of the young man who had emigrated to Africa—wanted to become a doctor, he had to go to the United States. He first attended Livingston College, in Salisbury, North Carolina. Livingston, a black college, was founded in 1879 by the African Methodist Episcopal Zion Church.

After receiving his bachelor's degree from Livingston, he attended Long Island College Hospital and Boston University, where he received his medical degree in 1897. In 1904, after years of working as a pathologist at Boston University, Dr. Fuller went to Germany to work with Alois Alzheimer at the University of Munich in the study of the degenerative nerve disease which later became known as Alzheimer's disease. He returned to the United States to teach and practice neurology and to become one of the first psychiatrists in America. The *Journal of the National Medical Association* in a tribute published in September 1954 noted that Dr. Fuller was best known for his studies in Alzheimer's disease and dementia.

Where Meta Warrick Fuller was playful and outgoing, Solomon Fuller was scholarly and studious, seeing even the most casual acquaintance as a possible source of knowledge. W.E.B. Du Bois was a frequent visit to the Fuller household, as was Harry Thacker Burleigh, the famed singer and composer. Solomon's son remembers that his father spent long hours listening to a man they occasionally hired to cart garbage away from their Framingham house. He liked to comb through old bookstores in Massachusetts and find good but damaged copies of books, which he would then carefully repair.

Used to the Liberian way of life, he had fully expected Meta to give up her sculpting when they married, but once it was clear that she did not wish to do so, he became one of her staunchest supporters. Dr. Fuller died in January 1953.

In New York's Harlem community there was an active arts movement which would become known as the Harlem Renaissance, but in Framingham there were very few African Americans, and Meta found herself isolated. Her work was being exhibited less and less frequently, and in 1910 she had much of it stored in a warehouse. A fire that destroyed the warehouse, and most of her work, put her in a deep depression.

Even so, Meta Warrick continued with her art. Most often the commissions she received were small ones, either from the government, when they specifically wanted an African-American sculptor, or from a black school or organization.

Her work *Awakening Ethiopia* was displayed at the Making of America Exposition in New York in 1922, and has been displayed in the Framingham library, the San Francisco Museum of Fine Arts, the Fine Arts Department of the Boston Public Library, and the Schomburg Library in New York City.

In her later life Meta Vaux Warrick Fuller turned increasingly to the poetry she loved.

I like Tennyson, Longfellow, I love Rossetti. . . . I have to dramatize everything I read. I get into the book. I'm one of the characters. It takes much longer to read if you do that. But the enjoyment is far greater than if you just read, read, read.

247

Meta Fuller was all that the United States could have asked of any of its citizens. She was bright, creative, and willing to contribute her talents to the building of America.

She and her husband had much in common. They both loved music and art. They were very much in love and lived a rich, full life together. But they had something else in common as well. Both had made the important decision to claim America as their home. Dr. Fuller's ancestors had been taken from Africa, been enslaved in America, and then recolonized in Liberia. Still he had come to the United States, even as Meta Warrick had returned from Paris, and both had given much of themselves to this country. Still, there were places where they could not sit down and eat a meal, or even drink a sip of water. *Plessy vs. Ferguson* had decided that issue for them. Nevertheless, they accomplished much by refusing to accept the limitations placed on them by racism.

Solomon C. Fuller, Jr., presently living on Cape Cod, Massachusetts, has fond memories of his childhood with Dr. Fuller and Meta Vaux Warrick Fuller. His mother, besides being a marvelous sculptor, was a wonderful parent. He still remembers their daily family suppers, the competition to spot the first robin of spring, the first sleigh of winter, and every sign of beauty that nature offered. He read me a poem that she had written, a poem that followed her resolve to accept the end of her life with as much grace as she had accepted the living.

Meta Vaux Warrick Fuller died March 13, 1968.

Departure
by Meta Vaux Warrick Fuller

The time is near (reluctance laid aside)
  I see the barque afloat upon the ebbing tide
While on the shores my friends and loved ones stand.
  I wave to them a cheerful parting hand,
Then take my place with Charon at the helm,
  And turn and wave again to them.
Oh, may the voyage not be arduous nor long,
  But echoing with chant and joyful song,
May I behold with reverence and grace,
  The wondrous vision of the Master's face.

22

Brown vs. Board of Education

There was a time when the meaning of freedom was easily understood. For an African crouched in the darkness of a tossing ship, wrists chained, men with guns standing on the decks above him, freedom was a physical thing, the ability to move away from his captors, to follow the dictates of his own heart, to listen to the voices within him that defined his values and showed him the truth of his own path. The plantation owners wanted to make the Africans feel helpless, inferior. They denied them images of themselves as Africans and told them that they were without beauty. They segregated them and told them they were without value.

Slowly, surely, the meaning of freedom changed to an elusive thing that even the strongest people could not hold in their hands. There were no chains on black wrists, but there were the shadows of chains, stretching for hundreds of years back through time, across black minds.

From the end of the Civil War in 1865 to the early 1950's, many public schools in both the North and South were segregated. Segregation was different in the different sections of the country. In the North most of the schools were segregated *de facto*; that is, the law allowed blacks and whites to go to school together, but they did not actually always attend the same schools. Since a school is generally attended by children living in its neighborhood, wherever there were predominantly African-American neighborhoods there were, "in fact," segregated schools. In many parts of the country, however, and especially in the South, the segregation was *de jure*, meaning that there were laws which forbade blacks to attend the same schools as whites.

The states with segregated schools relied upon the ruling of the Supreme Court in the 1896 *Plessy vs. Ferguson* case for legal justification: Facilities that were "separate but equal" were legal.

In the early 1950's the National Association for the Advancement of Colored People (N.A.A.C.P.) sponsored five cases that eventually reached the Supreme Court. One of the cases involved the school board of Topeka, Kansas.

Thirteen families sued the Topeka school board, claiming that to segregate the children was harmful to the children and, therefore, a violation of the equal protection clause of the Fourteenth Amendment. The names on the Topeka case were listed

251

in alphabetical order, with the father of seven-year-old Linda Brown listed first.

I didn't understand why I couldn't go to school with my playmates. I lived in an integrated neighborhood and played with children of all nationalities, but when school started they went to a school only four blocks from my home and I was sent to school across town,

she says.

For young Linda the case was one of convenience and of being made to feel different, but for African-American parents it had been a long, hard struggle to get a good education for their children. It was also a struggle waged by lawyers who had worked for years to overcome segregation. The head of the legal team who presented the school cases was Thurgood Marshall.

———

The city was Baltimore, Maryland, and the year was 1921. Thirteen-year-old Thurgood Marshall struggled to balance the packages he was carrying with one hand while he tried to get his bus fare out of his pocket with the other. It was almost Easter, and the part-time job he had would provide money for flowers for his mother. Suddenly he felt a violent tug at his right arm that spun him around, sending his packages sprawling over the floor of the bus.

"Nigguh, don't you never push in front of no white lady again!" an angry voice spat in his ear.

Thurgood turned and threw a punch into the face of the name caller. The man charged into Thurgood, throwing punches that mostly missed, and tried to wrestle the slim boy to the ground. A policeman broke up the fight, grabbing Thurgood with one huge black hand and pushing him against the side of the bus. Within minutes they were in the local courthouse.

Thurgood was not the first of his family to get into a good fight. His father's father had joined the Union Army during the Civil War, taking the names Thorough Good to add to the one name he had in bondage. His grandfather on his mother's side was a man brought from Africa and, according to Marshall's biography, "so ornery that his owner wouldn't sell him out of pity for the people who might buy him, but gave him his freedom instead and told him to clear out of the county."

Thurgood's frequent scrapes earned him a reputation as a young boy who couldn't be trusted to get along with white folks.

His father, Will Marshall, was a steward at the Gibson Island Yacht Club near Baltimore, and his mother, Norma, taught in a segregated school. The elder Marshall felt he could have done more with his life if his education had been better, but there had been few opportunities available for African Americans when he had been a young man. When it was time for the Marshall boys to go to college, he was more than willing to make the sacrifices necessary to send them.

Young people of color from all over the world came to the United States to study at Lincoln University, a predominantly black institution in southeastern Pennsylvania. Here Marshall majored in predentistry, which he found boring, and joined the Debating Club, which he found interesting. By the time he was graduated at the age of twenty-one, he had decided to give up dentistry for the law. Three years later he was graduated, first in his class, from Howard University Law School.

At Howard there was a law professor, Charles Hamilton Houston, who would affect the lives of many African-American lawyers and who would influence the legal aspects of the civil rights movement. Houston was a great teacher, one who demanded that his students be not just good lawyers but great lawyers. If they were going to help their people—and for Houston the only reason for African Americans to become lawyers was to do just that—they would have to have absolute understanding of the law, and be diligent in the preparation of their cases. At the time, Houston was an attorney for the N.A.A.C.P. and fought against discrimination in housing and in jobs.

After graduation, Thurgood Marshall began to do some work for the N.A.A.C.P., trying the difficult civil rights cases. He not only knew about the effects of discrimination by reading about it, he was still living it when he was graduated from law school in 1933. In 1936 Marshall began working full-time for the N.A.A.C.P., and in 1940 became its chief counsel.

It was Thurgood Marshall and a battery of N.A.A.C.P. attorneys who began to challenge segregation throughout the country. These men and women were warriors in the cause of freedom for African Americans, taking their battles into courtrooms across the country. They understood the process of American justice and the power of the Constitution.

Thurgood Marshall working on a civil rights case for the N.A.A.C.P. in 1952. *Library of Congress*

In *Brown vs. Board of Education of Topeka*, Marshall argued that segregation was a violation of the Fourteenth Amendment—that even if the facilities and all other "tangibles" were equal, which was the heart of the case in *Plessy vs. Ferguson*, a violation still existed. There were intangible factors, he argued, that made the education unequal.

Everyone involved understood the significance of the case: that it was much more than whether black children could go to school with white children. If segregation in the schools was declared unconstitutional, then *all* segregation in public places could be declared unconstitutional.

Southerners who argued against ending school segregation were caught up, as then-Congressman Brooks Hays of Arkansas put it, in "a lifetime of adventures in that gap between law and custom." The law was one thing, but most Southern whites felt just as strongly about their customs as they did the law.

Dr. Kenneth B. Clark, an African-American psychologist, testified for the N.A.A.C.P. He presented clear evidence that the effect of segregation was harmful to African-American children. Describing studies conducted by black and white psychologists over a twenty-year period, he showed that black children felt inferior to white children. In a particularly dramatic study that he had supervised, four dolls, two white and two black, were presented to African-American children. From the responses of the children to the dolls, identical in every way except color, it was clear that the children were rejecting the black dolls. African-American children did not just feel separated from white children, they felt that the separation was based on their inferiority.

Dr. Clark understood fully the principles and ideas of those people who had held Africans in bondage and had tried to make slaves of captives. By isolating people of African descent, by barring them from certain actions or places, they could make them feel inferior. The social scientists who testified at *Brown vs. Board of Education* showed that children who felt inferior also performed poorly.

The Justice Department argued that racial segregation was objectionable to the Eisenhower Administration and hurt our relationships with other nations.

On May 17, 1954, after deliberating for nearly a year and a half, the Supreme Court made its ruling. The Court stated that it could not use the intentions of 1868, when the Fourteenth Amendment was passed, as a guide to its ruling, or even those of 1896, when the decision in *Plessy vs. Ferguson* was handed down. Chief Justice Earl Warren wrote:

We must consider public education in the light of its full development and its present place in American life throughout the nation. We must look instead to the effect of segregation itself on public education.

The Court went on to say that "modern authority" supported the idea that segregation deprived African Americans of equal opportunity. "Modern authority" referred to Dr. Kenneth B. Clark and the weight of evidence that he and the other social scientists had presented.

The high court's decision in *Brown vs. Board of Education*

257

signaled an important change in the struggle for civil rights. It signaled clearly that the legal prohibitions that oppressed African Americans would have to fall. Equally important was the idea that the nature of the fight for equality would change. Ibrahima, Cinqué, Nat Turner, and George Latimer had struggled for freedom by fighting against their captors or fleeing from them. The 54th had fought for African freedom on the battlefields of the Civil War. Ida B. Wells had fought for equality with her pen. Lewis H. Latimer and Meta Vaux Warrick had tried to earn equality with their work. In *Brown vs. Board of Education* Thurgood Marshall, Kenneth B. Clark, and the lawyers and social scientists, both black and white, who helped them had won for African Americans a victory that would bring them closer to full equality than they had ever been in North America. There would still be legal battles to be won, but the major struggle would be in the hearts and minds of people and "in that gap between law and custom."

In 1967 Thurgood Marshall was appointed by President Lyndon B. Johnson as an associate justice of the U.S. Supreme Court. He retired in 1991.

"I didn't think of my father or the other parents as being heroic at the time," Linda Brown says. "I was only seven. But as I grew older and realized how far-reaching the case was and how it changed the complexion of the history of this country, I was just thrilled that my father and the others here in Topeka were involved."

23

Martin Luther King, Jr., and the Modern Civil Rights Movement

There are lessons too valuable to forget, moments in time so precious that they lift us above our everyday existence and give us to history. Such a time was the beginning of the civil rights movement in America. We need to remember its heroes and its villains. We need to remember the hundreds of marchers, footsore and weary but triumphant in the rightness of their cause. We need to remember the clergy and the cleaning women, the students and the bus drivers, the housewives, doctors, mechanics, and photographers who made the movement happen. We need to remember those who gave their lives that others might be free in America, and those who sat in humble kitchens praying for the safe return of the protestors, for the familiar step on the stair, the familiar voice to signal that all was well.

In some persons we find heroes, in some martyrs, in some

leaders, in some the symbolism of a time, and of a place. The modern civil rights movement began a century after the beginning of the Civil War. It took many forms and had many leaders; one of those leaders was Dr. Martin Luther King, Jr.

On October 19, 1960, a group of seventy-five students went to downtown Atlanta, Georgia, and launched what one journalist called "The Second Battle of Atlanta." They went into restaurants where African Americans were, by custom, not served, and they sat at the counters and at the tables. The store owners immediately understood that the students were organized and were challenging Southern segregation practices. The police were called and the participants of the sit-in, as it was quickly called, were arrested for trespassing. Among those arrested was a thirty-one-year-old minister named Martin Luther King, Jr.

King was taken to jail, where he was told that he would be released on $500 bail. Even though he could have put up the $500, to call attention to the injustice of the situation he decided to stay in jail.

Segregation in public schools had been declared unconstitutional by *Brown vs. Board of Education*, but the defeat in the courts did not stop the segregationists. President Eisenhower had expressed the sentiments of many people when he said, "It is difficult through law and through force to change a man's heart." A Civil Rights Act was passed in 1957, and an act providing protection of voting rights was passed in 1960. Still, angry

Dr. Martin Luther King, Jr., with his wife, Coretta Scott King. *New York Public Library, Schomburg Collection*

mobs continued to try to prevent integration in schools throughout the South.

A bus boycott in Montgomery, Alabama, had launched the
career of the Reverend Martin Luther King, Jr., who became the
spokesman for the nonviolent movement toward integration.
One of the strategies of the nonviolent movement was sit-ins.
People protesting segregation, primarily students, would sit in
areas reserved for "whites only" and allow themselves to be
arrested. Some communities had already accepted integration;
others had resisted it, sometimes with violence.

Senator John F. Kennedy of Massachusetts had his staff call
Mayor Hartsfield of Atlanta to see what could be done about
securing King's release. Mayor Hartsfield, looking for a peace-
ful solution to the conflict, promised the students that he would
attempt to negotiate with the merchants to desegregate the
downtown restaurants. The students were released, but King
was not. Neighboring DeKalb county asked that King be turned
over to them for violating probation. (In the previous spring he
had been convicted of driving with an invalid permit, fined $25,
and given a year's probation. His arrest for trespassing violated
that probation.) King was taken to the jail in DeKalb and, six
days later, sentenced to four months at hard labor. He was
denied bail, and his lawyers were told they had very little time
to appeal the case.

King asked his wife, Coretta, to bring him reading materials,
pens, and paper. She promised she would bring them the next
morning.

That night as King was lying in his bed, he was awakened by

someone shaking him. He turned away from the flashlight that shone in his eyes.

"Wake up! Wake up!" Several men hovered over him in the darkness of the cell.

He was pulled to his feet, pushed out of the cell, and told to shut up when he asked where he was being taken. Outside the cell he was hustled down the corridor, one of the men who had wakened him going before him and two more at his sides. He was taken to a small office, where he was handcuffed. The other men were already in jackets, and King tensed as he realized that he was being taken from the jail.

King knew what lynch law meant. He had known of other black men taken from jails in the middle of the night to be shot or hanged on lonely roads.

He asked again where he was being taken, and was again told to shut up. He was pushed into the back of a waiting car and a moment later was headed off into the darkness of a cool Georgia night.

The Sweet Auburn area of Atlanta was where Martin Luther King had been born on January 15, 1929, and where the Ebenezer Baptist Church, where he was co-pastor with his father, stood as the spiritual rock of the community. Somehow word got back to the Sweet Auburn district that King had been taken from the prison, and that no one knew where he was being taken. Everyone in the black community knew what the possibilities were. Some people began to pray, others gathered in small groups on the corners, others openly wept. The entire neighborhood was aroused; hurried phone calls were made to

Washington and to the governor's office. Radios were turned on as the neighborhood waited for word.

In the car King sat handcuffed in the back, his palms wet with perspiration, the handcuffs biting into his flesh as the car maneuvered on the dark country roads. Every car that pulled alongside terrified King; every stop made his heart race as he knew it could be his last. They drove for long hours, sometimes quickly, sometimes painfully slowly. At long last the car pulled up next to a brick wall and someone looked into the car. King was told to get out. His legs were weak as he stood. He looked up and saw that he was at Reidsville Penitentiary, over two hundred miles from Atlanta.

King stayed in the Reidsville Prison for two days and was suddenly released. He found out later that the Kennedys' staff had made the arrangements.

Not all the civil rights confrontations turned out so fortunately. There are always people who are more than willing to use violence against people dedicated to nonviolence, people willing to use intimidation against people who want only to be treated as equals.

What made the civil rights movement of the sixties different from earlier phases of the struggle was that it took place under the glare of the most extensive news coverage the world had ever known. When a civil rights leader was injured or killed, it was not simply whispered—it was front-page headlines. People

Dorothy Counts integrating the previously all-white Harding High School in Charlotte, North Carolina, in 1957. *UPI/Bettmann Archive* who resorted to violence found themselves on front pages and on the evening news. What's more, it was violence that by now most people, white and black, North and South, did not think was right.

The media coverage also prompted more and more people to participate in the movement. Busloads of students, clergy, workers, and housewives joined new sit-ins, not only at lunch counters but in bus terminals and other public areas.

While in the South Martin Luther King, Jr., was leading the nonviolent move to integrate American society, Malcolm X in the North was preaching a different philosophy.

Malcom X was born Malcolm Little in Omaha, Nebraska, on May 19, 1925, and grew up in Lansing, Michigan. His father died when he was a small child, and his mother was hospitalized shortly after. In Lansing he saw his home burned down by the Ku Klux Klan. Malcolm was put into a series of foster homes, finally ending up on the streets of New York when he was fifteen. He was arrested in 1946 for robbery and sent to prison. It was in prison that Malcolm Little was introduced to the Nation of Islam and became part of that movement.

He dropped what he called his "slave" name, feeling that it represented captivity: Most African Americans' surnames were those of their one-time masters. The Black Muslims, as the members of the Nation of Islam were called, preached racial separation, racial pride, and economic independence. While

Malcolm X. *Michael Ochs Archives*

Martin Luther King insisted on a nonviolent philosophy as the only viable strategy, Malcolm X sought full equality by "any means possible."

Malcolm X believed in the Islamic religion, made a pilgrimage to Mecca, and changed his name to Al Hajj Malik al-Shabazz. In his later years he accepted the idea that black liberation could be helped by a variety of world organizations, and embraced for the first time the possibility of a world brotherhood that included people of all races and nationalities. Still he maintained his belief that African Americans should be armed against white violence.

Malcolm X responded to King's message of love by saying that whites loved blacks as slaves and the only way to get them to love blacks again was to be a slave again.

King responded to Malcolm X's message of violence.

I feel that Malcolm has done himself and our people a great disservice. Fiery, demagogic oratory in the black ghettos, urging Negroes to arm themselves and prepare to engage in violence, as he has done, can reap nothing but grief.

Most African-American leaders decided that Martin Luther King's philosophy best fit the need of the times. Many young people, however, were more attracted to Malcolm X's militancy.

The civil rights movement took place largely in the South because the first goal of the movement, human dignity, was most affronted there. But the treatment of African Americans in the North was, in many cases, worse than in the South. The laws in the South spoke of racial division, but the actuality of the North showed little, if any, difference. While schools were not legally segregated in the North, most schools were in fact nearly segregated in the early fifties. While it was easy for blacks to vote in cities like New York and Chicago, that vote brought little real empowerment. Neighborhoods were segregated not by law, but by "gentlemen's agreements." It was infinitely easier to get Northern support to fight segregation in the South than it was to fight segregation in the North.

On August 28, 1963, there was a nationwide march on Washington. People from all over the country, from the South and from the North, converged on the nation's capital. Dr. King gave a speech that would be long remembered.

I have a dream that one day this nation will rise up and live out the true meaning of its creed, "We hold these truths to be self-evident, that all men are created equal." I have a dream that one day on the red hills of Georgia, the sons of former slaves and the sons of former slave owners will be able to sit down together at the table of brotherhood.

Dr. Martin Luther King continued his crusade for civil rights until April 4, 1968. On that day he was in Memphis, Tennessee, to support the black sanitation workers of that city, who were on strike. He was standing on the balcony of the Lorraine Hotel talking to some friends in the parking lot below when a rifle shot resounded through the small complex. Martin Luther King, Jr., fell, mortally wounded.

Dr. King was not the target of the assassin. The dreams of African Americans for freedom and equality were the true target. The bullet missed. Dr. King was killed, but the dreams lived on.

The sixties were years marked by violence and hate. Malcolm X was assassinated, as were President John F. Kennedy and his brother Robert, and civil rights workers, white and black.

Dr. King was a man. When he walked, his feet touched the ground. When he lifted his arms, they did not reach the heavens. But he was a man for a time and for a place. He brought the struggle for equality into the world spotlight as no one had before him.

The civil rights movement of the sixties was, to a large degree, a triumph for America, for in many ways America did what most societies have not been able to do: It changed. It changed from a society in which there was no doubt that one section of its population was forever doomed to subservient status to a society in which virtually everyone was beginning to have a chance for life, liberty, and the pursuit of happiness.

The sixties also gave us something else precious to remember: the story of people willing to risk their lives so that others could go to schools of their choice, could vote for candidates of their choice, and could hold their heads up with pride, whatever race they were. Some of these people we know well; countless others will be forgotten.

There were thousands of African-American women who led marches, who went to jails, who served late suppers, who were hard as stone when they needed to be hard, who brought their quiet support and incredible courage to the struggle, and who continue to do so as the struggle continues.

There were young people, white and black, who marched and sang and prayed together. There were older people, white and black, from the South and from the North, who stood up when it would have been so much easier, so much safer, to be quiet.

We have not forgotten those who have lived to bear witness to the fight for human dignity, or those who gave their lives that others might enjoy the full promise of America; they have just assumed a different place in our history.

Those who have lived to bear witness to the struggles of the past are our guides to who we are; those who have joined the ancestors are no less alive in either the struggle or the rich culture of our people. We are each of us forever linked to our own history, each of us a beginning and each a going on.

Afterword

Who are we really, we who call ourselves African Americans? To begin with we are people, like Ibrahima, of African descent. Each of our forebears has come from a culture that knew learning, government, art, religion, and appreciation of our humanity. If Africa seems distant, then it has been made so by our neglect. But if we listen closely to its rhythms, if we look at its art, we will find the echoes that link us with our heritage.

Like our elders held in bondage, we know suffering and know that we can persevere, for our limbs are strong and our spirits stronger yet. When there is nothing around us that speaks of salvation, we have found it within, blessed in the knowledge that we are not alone, but are a people.

Like James Forten we are lovers of liberty. We are a people who have defended the freedom not only of the United States but of the world. Our blood has been shed in the Revolutionary War, the War of 1812, the Civil War, the Spanish-American War, the First and Second World Wars, Korea, Vietnam, and the Persian Gulf. We have not shrunk from the call to defend the nation we call home.

Like George Latimer we are a people who understand that there is no chance too desperate, no road too perilous if it leads to freedom. Like Lewis H. Latimer, his son, we are a people of industry and genius, delighted in the beauty of our kind and in ourselves.

Like the soldiers of the 54th we are brave. We have charged fiercely, bayonets fixed, into the face of oppression, and we have waited for it in the blaze of noon and on sultry summer nights with only our bare hands to defend us and the comfort of knowing that a just world can exist.

Like Ida B. Wells we have spoken out against injustice when it would have been so much easier, so much safer, to be quiet. And we have spoken out boldly and eloquently, and we have not grown tired.

Like Meta Vaux Warrick Fuller we have brought our art to the world and used it as a weapon against our enemies, and as a token of love for those who would accept it.

Like Thurgood Marshall we have prepared ourselves well and have been profound in our understanding, determined to survive the scorn of our detractors.

Like Malcolm X we have grown impatient with promises and weary with waiting for the love we send out to be returned.

Like Martin Luther King we have been to the mountaintop,

273

glimpsing the full freedom that America has to offer, confident in our path and in our vision.

We are a people capable of understanding our own nobility, and our own failures. We have seen who we can be and know that those who have gone before us, who lived their lives well so that we might be free, would demand that we be no less than we can be.

An ancient symbol in Ghana is the Sankofa bird. "Sankofa" means to turn back and get what you have left behind. The people of Ghana use it to remind themselves that before you can go forward, you must know where you have been.

Gold weight from Ghana in the form of the Sankofa bird. *Author*

Author's Note

Separating the facts from the fictions of African-American history is an arduous but ultimately rewarding endeavor. Some facts are relatively easy to check. The records of Ibrahima's being bought by Foster are still on file in Mississippi, as is the American Colonization Society record of his return to Africa shortly before his death.

The search for James Forten led me to the rare books room of the New York Public Library, where I found newspapers from Philadelphia in 1781 and the name of a researcher in England who provided the log books of the British vessel *Amphyon*.

More difficult, however, was trying to determine whether the crops produced by plantation owners were meant for sale or for maintenance of the plantation population. When there was no cash crop but a large African population, the chief "crop" of the plantation was often the Africans themselves. For help in determining the probable use of crops, the Agriculture Department of the University of Kansas was invaluable.

I was raised by foster parents, so tracing my own "roots" was particularly interesting. The Dandridges, who held part of my family in bondage before the Civil War, were prominent enough to find easily through census, court, and tax records. Starting with the National Archives, I could easily trace part of my ancestral tree back to the Dandridge plantation, all the time wondering if my findings would confirm the oral history that had passed from generation to generation in my family. They did. The records in the West Virginia Collection at the University of West Virginia were filled with prominent names of people and places, names that had bounced around my family living room for years.

Sometimes my research only deepened the confusion. For example, the records at the American Baptist Society at first indicated that the Baptists had established the Free Will Baptist Church in Martinsburg, West Virginia, my birthplace. My sisters said that no such church existed. The discrepancy was cleared up when we both discovered that the official name of the church my family had always called "Dudley Baptist" was indeed Free Will Baptist.

The most interesting aspect of the research was the people. Listening to Winifred Latimer Norman talking about her grandfather, Lewis Howard Latimer, as I looked through his papers was thrilling. Solomon Fuller not only shared his memories of his parents and the oral history that had been part of his family;

he also brought me to a much greater understanding of the early African-American middle class, as well as what he called the "value of cultural substance" present in the true ethnicity of all peoples. I was glad to be able to document, from Library of Congress records, some of his family's interesting history.

The middle-grade students in my writing workshop helped me formulate my questions to Linda Brown of *Brown vs. Board of Education.* She, in turn, cleared up many previously published misconceptions about her role in the celebrated Supreme Court case.

I met Thurgood Marshall only once, and that briefly at the NAACP Legal Defense Fund in New York, but the experience was a memorable one that helped me to understand this fine man.

I walked about the Sweet Auburn district where Martin Luther King worked and lived, and I talked to people who shared their memories of Malcolm X. I stood in the engine house that held John Brown's raiders and traced the smooth lines of the sides of the wagon that carried him to his execution.

I bought photographs and documents from sources across the country in an attempt to get as close to the actual events as I could. Often the research was incredibly rewarding, sometimes it was painful, but it always brought me closer to understanding what has been my history.

Select Bibliography

General

Bennett, Lerone, Jr. *Before the Mayflower: A History of Black America.* Chicago: Johnson Publishing Co., 1987.

Franklin, John Hope. *From Slavery to Freedom.* New York: Vintage Books, 1969.

Sobel, Michael. *The World They Made Together.* Princeton, NJ: Princeton University Press, 1987.

Africa

Ajayi, J. F. Ade. *General History of Africa.* Paris: United Nations Educational, Scientific and Cultural Organization, 1989.

Brooks, Lester. *Great Civilizations of Ancient Africa.* New York: Four Winds Press, 1971.

McEwan, P.J.M. *Africa From Early Times to 1800.* London: Oxford University Press, 1968.

Plantation Life

Greenberg, Kenneth S. *Masters and Statesmen.* Baltimore: The Johns Hopkins University Press, 1985.

Helper, Hinton Rowan. *The Impending Crisis.* New York: Burdick Brothers, 1857.

Land, Aubrey C. *Bases of the Plantation Society.* New York: Harper & Row, 1969.

Phillips, Ulrich B. *Life and Labor in the Old South.* Boston: Little, Brown and Company, 1929.

———. *Plantation and Frontier Documents.* New York: Burt Franklin, 1910, 1969.

African Captivity

Breeden, James O. *Advice Among Masters: The Ideal in Slave Management in the Old South.* Westport, CT: Greenwood Press, 1980.

Mullin, Michael. *American Negro Slavery.* Columbia, SC: University of South Carolina Press, 1976.

Rawley, James A. *The Trans-Atlantic Slave Trade.* New York: W. W. Norton & Company, 1981.

Rose, Willie Lee. *A Documentary History of Slavery in North America.* New York: Oxford University Press, 1976.

Tadman, Michael. *Speculators and Slaves.* Madison, WI: University of Wisconsin Press, 1989.

Woodman, Harold D. *Slavery and the Southern Economy.* San Diego: Harcourt Brace Jovanovich, Publishers, 1966.

Abd al-Rahman Ibrahima

Alford, Terry. *Prince Among Slaves.* New York: Oxford University Press, 1977.

American Colonization Society. "Abduhl Rahahman's History." *African Repository* (February, May, June 1828).

James Forten

Kaplan, Sidney, and Emma Nogrady. *The Black Presence in the Era of the American Revolution.* Amherst, MA: University of

Massachusetts Press, 1989.

Livermore, Charles. *Negroes as Slaves, Citizens, and Soldiers.* New York: Burt Franklin, 1862.

Nell, William C. *Colored Patriots of the American Revolution.* New York. Arno Press, 1968.

Formation of the United States of America

Blum, John M.; William S. McFeely; Edmund S. Morgan; Arthur M. Schlesinger, Jr.; Kenneth M. Stampp; and C. Vann Woodward. *The National Experience.* San Diego: Harcourt Brace Jovanovich, Publishers, 1988.

Morison, Samuel Eliot. *The Oxford History of the American People.* New York: Oxford University Press, 1965.

The Latimers

Davis, Asa J. "The Two Autobiographical Fragments of George W. Latimer (1820–1896): A Preliminary Assessment." *Journal of the Afro-American Historical and Genealogical Society.*

Haber, Louis. *Black Pioneers of Science and Invention.* San Diego: Harcourt Brace Jovanovich, Publishers, 1970.

Nat Turner

Drewery, William S. *Southampton Insurrection.* Washington, DC: Neale Company, 1900.

Tragle, Henry Irving. *The Nat Turner Slave Revolt.* New York: Grossman Publishers, 1972.

John Brown

Anderson, Osbourne P. *A Voice from Harper's Ferry.* New York: World View Publishers, 1974.

Barry, Joseph. *The Strange Incident in Harper's Ferry.* Martinsburg, WV: Thompson Brothers, 1903.

Federal Writer's Project, Manuscript Collection. University of West Virginia Collection. Morgantown, WV.

Villard, Oswald Garrison. *John Brown.* New York: Alfred A. Knopf, Inc., 1943.

The Civil War

Appleton, John. The Diary of John Appleton, microfilm. University of West Virginia Collection. Morgantown, WV.

Emilio, Luis F. *History of the Fifty-fourth Regiment.* Boston: The Boston Book Company, 1894.

Forten, Charlotte. *The Journal of Charlotte L. Forten.* New York: Collier Books, 1961.

Thomas, Emory M. *Bold Dragoon.* New York: Harper & Row, 1986.

Von Borcke, Heros. *Memoirs of the Confederate War for Independence.* New York: Peter Smith, 1938.

Williams, Ben Ames. *A Diary From Dixie: Mary Boykin Chesnut.* Cambridge, MA: Harvard University Press, 1980.

Reconstruction

Eby, Cecil D. *Porte Crayon: The Life of David Hunter Strother.* Chapel Hill, NC: University of North Carolina Press, 1960.

Wells, Ida B. *Crusade for Justice.* Chicago: University of Chicago Press, 1970.

The Fullers

Kerr, Judith Nina. "Meta Fuller." Unpublished thesis. Amherst, MA: University of Massachusetts, 1987.

The Studio Museum in Harlem, New York. *Harlem Renaissance.* New York: Harry N. Abrams, Inc., 1987.

Civil Rights

Branch, Taylor. *Parting the Waters: America in the King Years 1954–1963.* New York: Simon & Schuster, Inc., 1988.

Clark, Kenneth B. *Prejudice and Your Child.* Boston: Beacon Press, 1955.

Fenderson, Lewis H. *Thurgood Marshall, Fighter for Justice.* New York: McGraw-Hill, Inc., 1969.

Haley, Alex. *The Autobiography of Malcolm X.* New York: Grove Press, Inc., 1965.

Lomax, Louis E. *When the Word Is Given.* Cleveland: The World Publishing Company, 1963.

Index

Numbers in *italics* refer to illustrations.

288

15 WEST END

J 973.0496 MYERS   WEB
Myers, Walter Dean
Now is your time!

Atlanta-Fulton Public Library

R00667 52144   MAY 1 2 1992